When my children were young, it all fel
do *everything* right or make HUGE, dra
make my sons grow into the men of Go
a lot of pressure for one mom to carry, a
to be that way. I'm so grateful to Christie ... breaking it down for us into
smaller pieces that when put together help point our families to Jesus.

BROOKE McGLOTHLIN, founder of Million Praying Moms and host of the
Everyday Prayers with Million Praying Moms podcast

As always, Christie is insightful, helpful, and encouraging. If you're a
Christian parent, you can't go wrong with *Little Habits, Big Faith*!

RYAN COATNEY, founder of Cross Formed Kids and pastor of Grace Story Church

No matter your level of experience with family discipleship or the age
of your children, this book will help you build even better discipleship
habits. After establishing the value of the parent's role, Christie
Thomas shows parents—step-by-step—how to leave behind legalism
and nurture their children into joy-filled faith. Short, thorough, and
practical, this book is a reliable primer for someone who wants to learn
how to disciple their children.

ELIZABETH SANTELMANN, host of the *Sunshine in My Nest* podcast

Christie is one of the most trusted and honest thought leaders in family
ministry. In her latest offering, you'll find a nonanxious, down-to-earth
conversation partner for this stretch of the road known as parenting.
This book is highly practical while carefully steering away from being
a manual for how things must be done. I can't wait to recommend this
grace-filled, hopeful book to parents for years to come!

CHRIS AMMEN, founder of Kaleidoscope

Finally, a parenting book that I'm excited about! Christie Thomas offers
a step-by-step guide to passing on the faith that feels not only doable but
fun. Her witty charm and personal storytelling will make parents feel
seen, understood, and inspired to establish family rhythms of faith in
bite-sized portions. If you've felt overwhelmed by the pressure to do "all
the things," be encouraged: *Little Habits, Big Faith* was written for you.

MICHELLE REYES, PhD, professor of cultural engagement at Wheaton College
and award-winning author of *Becoming All Things*

Christie Thomas has written a highly readable and doable guide to cultivating faith in the next generation of children. Without being legalistic or formulaic, she plots out a highly organic pathway of habits that guides both parents and children. She is realistic with the problems parents encounter yet offers good resources and a lot of hope for the discouraged. She concludes chapters with testimonials from others and concludes her book with some valuable resources for follow-up. I wish this had been available in my parenting years, but it is also useful for grandparents to tap into.

> DON HARDER, MA, retired pastor and superintendent, Evangelical Free Church of Canada

If you love God and his Word, you ache to raise kids who do too. Yet this task can feel overwhelming, and the results may seem uncertain. Christie Thomas is someone I trust to provide parents with everything they need to communicate biblical principles to their kids in warm and inviting ways. *Little Habits, Big Faith* will give you a good start on this process and a hand to hold along the journey. Christie's experience in children's ministry and parenting spills over into this beautiful book. Learn from her, and apply what you learn. Nothing could be more important!

> MONICA SWANSON, author of *Boy Mom* and *Raising Amazing* and host of *The Monica Swanson Podcast*

Doable! *Little Habits, Big Faith* offers parents a practical, relatable, and easily applicable approach to discipling their children. Author Christie Thomas understands that one size does not fit all. The strategies she suggests can be uniquely tailored to any family. This book will assist you in partnering with God to intentionally grow big faith in your kids through making small yet impactful adjustments. With Christie's guidance, you can do it!

> LORI WILDENBERG, licensed parent and family educator and author of six parenting books, including *The Messy Life of Parenting: Powerful and Practical Ways to Strengthen Family Connections*

Every family needs this book! Christie is so good at taking big, overwhelming concepts and breaking them down so parents can implement faith habits in everyday life. I own every one of Christie's books, and I'm so delighted with the insight and practical wisdom in *Little Habits, Big Faith.*

ERICKA ANDERSEN, author of *Reason to Return: Why Women Need the Church and the Church Needs Women*

So often in parenting and discipling our kids, we get in our own way and we worry about teaching all the right things or we focus on our limitations. In *Little Habits, Big Faith*, Christie reminds us that faith development happens in relationships and encourages us that we are not alone in any of the struggles we go through as we raise our kids to know and love Jesus. But instead of a long list of to-dos, Christie offers us simple habits that only take thirty seconds and will change our family's faith. I promise you will not finish this book feeling overwhelmed, unequipped, or discouraged. You will finish this book feeling confident that little by little, moment by moment, you *can* help your kids develop a meaningful and deep faith in Jesus that will last a lifetime.

STEPH THURLING, coauthor of *Raising Prayerful Kids*, executive director of Christian Parenting, and host of *The Christian Parenting Podcast*

If you're exhausted from Christian parenting approaches that make you feel like you have to "get it right," *Little Habits, Big Faith* will refresh your weary soul. Christie Thomas offers us a better way to disciple and build foundations of faith with our children. Demonstrating the freedom to custom-fit Christian parenting to our own unique families, Christie shows how to weave faith into the everyday, small moments of life. *Little Habits, Big Faith* shows parents how they can have peace in the process of training their children in the Lord and focus on the part of discipleship that matters most—knowing and loving Jesus.

TERI McKINLEY, coauthor of the bestselling book *Our Daily Bread for Kids*

In *Little Habits, Big Faith*, Christie applies the science of habits to faith formation in a way that makes family discipleship feel easy, doable, and sustainable for every family, all while sharing encouragement and support. *Little Habits, Big Faith* addresses common roadblocks to family discipleship and shares perspective shifts and next steps for overcoming those struggles. Christie gives us a starting place for simple but effective family discipleship and then walks us deeper into guiding our kids to own their faith so discipleship becomes a lifelong journey for the entire family.

BRITTANY NELSON, author of *Time to Update: 7 Areas to Integrate Digital Discipleship into Your Children's Ministry Strategy* and creator of DeeperKidMin.com

This is the book every Christian parent needs to read. I was shouting "Amen!" after practically every sentence. Christie is relatable, honest, and helpful—the perfect guide to any modern, busy, slightly chaotic Christian parent who desires to disciple their kids. *Little Habits, Big Faith* manages to be down-to-earth about the realities of family life while also being aspirational about how we can journey toward Jesus together. There's not a single word here that didn't encourage me that I, too, could start small and grow big faith. Thank you, Christie—this is the family discipleship guide we all need in the 2020s.

LUCY RYCROFT, author, ministry lead at Parenting for Faith, and blogger at The Hope-Filled Family

In *Little Habits, Big Faith*, Christie Thomas reminds us that it's never too late to start small! This book is full of grace, gospel centered, and *deeply* practical. Using a biblically and psychologically informed approach to discipleship and habit formation, this work manages to provide detailed and specific guidance without being formulaic. Christie affirms the uniqueness of each family and structures *Little Habits, Big Faith* to help parents discern how to approach their children's spiritual formation in a way that is sustainable and life-giving. This encouraging and gentle resource is sure to bless Christian parents raising children of all ages.

DANIELLE HITCHEN, author of *Sacred Seasons* and the Baby Believer series

I want to buy a copy of this book for every parent I know! This book helps you understand the *why* behind raising your kids to know and love Jesus. It puts a fire in your bones and a passion in your heart to prioritize what matters most as you parent, but it also practically lays out how to make it happen in a way that is simple and will work for your unique family. Christie addresses the fears, roadblocks, and unrealistic expectations we come across as parents and helps us pray, confess, and start smaller so that our little habits can change the way we live! This is a powerful handbook to guide you as you bless, pray for, connect with, and disciple your kids. This is one I want to revisit again and again as I parent. I love all her ideas for little steps that lead to big, life-changing family habits.

SARAH HOLMSTROM, coauthor of *Raising Prayerful Kids*

No family functions the same as another. *Little Habits, Big Faith* allows for this fact and so much more. With realistic goals and ideas for how you can create a vision for your family, Christie gently leads you on a journey that makes discipleship feel possible and sustainable.

REBECCA RUYBALID STONE, author of *Discipleship for Kids: Helping Children Grow in Christ*

Dive into *Little Habits, Big Faith* and unlock a treasure trove of wisdom! Christie Thomas seamlessly weaves together research and personal experiences, offering parents and caregivers a road map to nurturing faith in children. With a straightforward three-step process, Thomas tackles the common stresses and insecurities of parenthood, providing practical solutions that promise growth not only for kids but for the entire family. This book is a must-read for anyone seeking to cultivate a thriving, faith-filled environment at home.

TERESA ROBERTS, DMIN, professor and author of *Raising Disciples: Guiding Your Kids into a Faith of Their Own*

As a pastor and father, I see challenges that result when families neglect to have a rule of life, the discerned and decided ways that we commit to following Jesus in our families. Through *Little Habits, Big Faith*, Christie Thomas not only addresses why we need a vision of faith in our families but also offers an encouraging and practical guide for how we, as parents, can kneel down into the soil and partner with God in the garden work already happening in the hearts of our children. Every parent will find something helpful and spiritually relevant for their family in *Little Habits, Big Faith*.

CRIS HARPER, lead pastor of Bethel Community Church

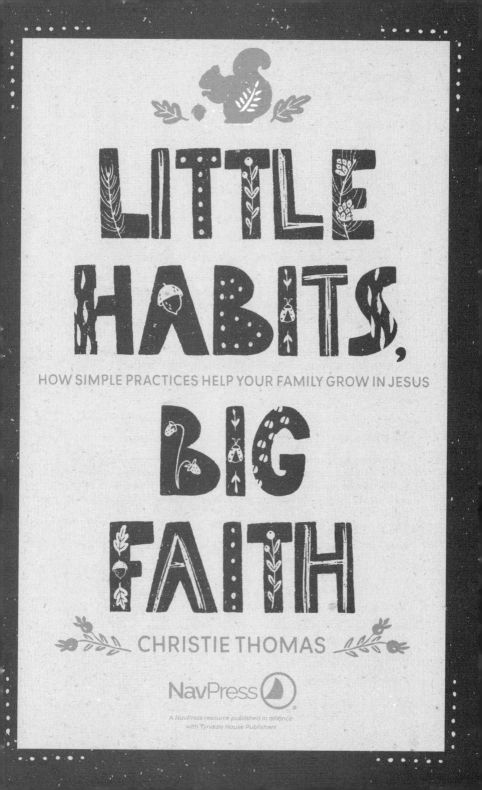

LITTLE HABITS,

HOW SIMPLE PRACTICES HELP YOUR FAMILY GROW IN JESUS

BIG FAITH

CHRISTIE THOMAS

NavPress®

A NavPress resource published in alliance
with Tyndale House Publishers

NavPress.com

A NavPress resource published in alliance with Tyndale House Publishers

NavPress and the NavPress logo are registered trademarks of NavPress, The Navigators, Colorado Springs, CO. *Tyndale* is a registered trademark of Tyndale House Ministries. Absence of ® in connection with marks of NavPress or other parties does not indicate an absence of registration of those marks.

The Team:
David Zimmerman, Publisher; Caitlyn Carlson, Senior Editor; Elizabeth Schroll, Copyeditor; Olivia Eldredge, Operations Manager; Julie Chen, Designer

Cover illustration of squirrel copyright © by Maggie Molloy/Creative Market. All rights reserved.

Typeface Forest Vibes copyright © by Moolesya/Creative Market. All rights reserved.

Author photo copyright © 2023 by Jonathon Thomas. All rights reserved.

Author is represented by the literary agency of Credo Communications LLC, Grand Rapids, Michigan, credocommunications.net

For information about special discounts for bulk purchases, please contact Tyndale House Publishers at csresponse@tyndale.com, or call 1-855-277-9400.

ISBN 978-1-64158-767-9

Printed in the United States of America

30	29	28	27	26	25	24
7	6	5	4	3	2	1

To the women of HopeGrown Faith:
You are the reason I'm brave enough to write for adults.

 A LITTLE BLESSING

As you tend the little and big ones in your care,

may you remain connected to the Vine,

allowing the Gardener to prune

so your life becomes a place

where the little habits

lead to deep roots

and big fruit,

for God's

glory.

CONTENTS

A VERY GOOD PLACE TO START

MY SON AND I ARE CURLED UP in the top bunk, surrounded by piles of stuffed animals and books, doing our bedtime routine. As we sing our memory verse together, he leans toward my ear and bats his eyelashes. (He thinks it's hilarious, but I feel like there's a moth in my ear. Ew.)

> When the kindness and love of God our Savior
> appeared, he saved us, not because of righteous things
> we had done, but because of his mercy. He saved us
> through the washing of rebirth and renewal by the
> Holy Spirit, whom he poured out on us generously
> through Jesus Christ our Savior, so that, having been
> justified by his grace, we might become heirs having
> the hope of eternal life.
>
> TITUS 3:4-7, NIV

There are some awfully big words in that verse, I realize. What does *justified* mean, anyway? I decide to explain: "*Justified* means that God doesn't see our sins anymore; he sees us through Jesus. That's what it means to be saved." And then I say, "Do you know what you need to do to be saved? Just say, 'Jesus, I want to be saved!'"

I'm chuckling inside at my simple explanation, but he takes it seriously. A second later, he tells me, "I just said that to Jesus, in my head!" He giggles, and I notice a new brightness in his eyes. For the first time—without pushing or prompting or pressure—he has made a personal profession of faith.* He wants to follow Jesus. I give him a squishy cry-hug, and he pats my back in amusement.

Life-changing moments with our kids can come out of simple habits. Tiny, intentional practices have helped me pay attention to the organic moments when God has been nudging me to take the conversation one step further. Would my son's lightbulb realization have happened without our regular rhythm of singing a bedtime verse together? Would I have noticed the opportunity to take that thirty-second habit one step further if I hadn't seen what God had done in other small moments of intentionality? Maybe. God can do anything he wants. But I believe that God used my stumbling faithfulness and a simple bedtime habit to bring my son into a true relationship with him.

And it all began with starting little.

---

* What is salvation? It involves (a) recognizing that we need saving because our sins separate us from God and (b) believing that the Savior we need is Jesus. "If you openly declare that Jesus is Lord and believe in your heart that God raised him from the dead, you will be saved. For it is by believing in your heart that you are made right with God, and it is by openly declaring your faith that you are saved. As the Scriptures tell us, 'Anyone who trusts in him will never be disgraced'" (Romans 10:9-11).

TWO TEAMS

Wondering what it looks like to start little—and how that's any different from the try-harder, do-all-the-things faith development you're used to hearing about?

Let's play a game. Imagine you're watching the end credits of a VeggieTales show with your kids when suddenly Bob the Tomato bounces onto the screen and says, "Hey, parents! Want to win an all-expenses-paid trip to a destination of your choice? This prize goes to the first family who gets into a habit of reading the Bible together every day!" (If you're not familiar with Bob and his fellow animated preaching produce, these characters have been teaching kids truths about the Bible since I was a teenager. Some of their silly songs are permanently in the soundtrack of my high school memories.)

What would you do in response to that challenge?

Option one is to join the all-out team. If you're following the method this team uses, you might

- hop online and order three new devotional books, hoping to find the right fit for your kids;
- hustle harder in the mornings, hoping to have time to read a devotion to your kids; and
- ask your kids ten times to sit and listen quietly at bedtime, until one of them starts rolling around on the floor and the teenager is rolling his eyes.

On the all-out team, we're working our butts off to keep kids engaged, but nothing seems to hold their attention. This method tends to leave us stressed and frustrated because they don't seem interested or aren't grasping the concepts. We lose steam because we don't want to push our kids away by shoving something down their throats. Occasionally we work up the energy to get going again because we know it's important, but it's tough to stay motivated because we keep receiving the same poor response from our kids.

The other approach? Step on over to the bit-by-bit team. If you're following the method this team uses, you might

- not start right away, but instead stop to pray about the best time and place to start a habit;
- choose a short, engaging passage from the Bible to begin with; and
- give your kids time and space to wiggle and interact with the Bible in their own way so everyone feels like they enjoyed the time together.

On the bit-by-bit team, you can hop off the guilt-ridden hamster wheel and live in freedom, knowing that you're fulfilling your calling to share your faith with your family without having to know it all or do it all.

And if you haven't joined a team yet and aren't sure if you need to do anything more than expose your children to church? Leaning into bit-by-bit changes can help you nix the fear that you'll manipulate them into faith. You can grow an open, positive relationship with your children while slowly helping them weave an authentic, Christ-centered faith.

Here's the thing: Most of us long for our kids to have a real, lifelong relationship with God. We don't need a talking tomato to offer us free trips as motivation, but we do wonder if we're doing enough, if we're doing it right, and how to move toward our goal of helping our kids connect more deeply with Jesus.

As I've tried to share my Christian faith with my kids, I've spent a lot of time on the all-out team. I might have even been the captain for a while.

When I began having kids, I read endless numbers of parenting books and family faith–development blogs, but eventually all that just made me want to back away and rock in a corner. I was so tired of being told I had to do all the things to be a "good Christian mom." Was I really failing if I didn't hold regular worship sessions with my kids and say in-depth prayers and read chapters of the Bible and memorize a verse a week and know the answers to every theological question and have my kids do workbook-style Bible studies? (I'm exhausted just writing that sentence.) And since I couldn't do all the things, was I messing up my boys for eternity?

Each book I read made me feel more and more overwhelmed. But simply shrugging off the guilt and not doing anything wasn't an option. I wanted to do *something*—but what could I do that was attainable . . . and still helped me and my kids grow more toward Christ? I knew there had to be a better way.

SMALL HABITS, POWERFUL CHANGES

Where I live, in the North Pole (kidding . . . sort of), we joke that we only have two seasons: winter and construction—otherwise known as "the making of the potholes" and "the fixing of the potholes." Through autumn, winter, and spring, small amounts of melted snow find their way into microscopic cracks in the road. Every time the temperature falls below freezing, that water turns into ice. If you've ever put a glass container of soup in the freezer, you know what happens when water turns to ice: It expands. Soup freezing in a too-small container can break glass, and water freezing in those cracks in the road can break asphalt. After eight months of the thaw-freeze-thaw-freeze cycle, you end up with huge potholes and cracks in the road.

When I finally admitted that my all-out method of family faith wasn't working, here's what God began to show me: Just as a few dribbles of water have the power to crack open a solid road, small but consistent choices have the power to crack into a busy routine and change the terrain of my family's faith.

If you're feeling weighed down and exhausted by all the things you're supposed to do to teach your children about God, I invite you to join me on the bit-by-bit team, whose methods we'll discover in this book. We're going to look at why our investment matters, what hasn't been working, and why we're feeling stuck. And then we're going to explore the way through: a simple process to establish family rhythms of faith and equip kids to grow a faith of their own called the Faith Growth Cycle. As we walk this path, we're going to discover the power of small, consistent choices: attainable, life-giving daily habits God can use to change how your family grows in faith.

This is a parenting book for people who don't like formulas. I will give you many ideas for how to invest in your kids' faith development, but you won't find copy-and-paste approaches here. I won't tell you to homeschool, homestead, or be a home-maker, though there's nothing wrong with any of those choices. Instead, I hope to help you sit at the feet of Jesus, along with your family, and learn what *he* wants for your unique family. Jesus is the only way to salvation, but the way each family faithfully follows him is going to look different, unique to the people, personalities, and positions God has given them. We're going to be exploring the *how* of spiritual formation so you're equipped to create the habits the Holy Spirit wants for you, instead of replicating someone else's plan.

This book is for you if

a. you want to read the Bible (or engage in any kind of faith-formation activity) with your kids in a way that clicks with them and doesn't make you want to pull your hair out;

b. you want to find consistent times to talk about faith with your kids without adding to your overflowing to-do list; and

c. you want your kids to trust in Jesus as their Lord and Savior.

Nothing we do will guarantee our kids will choose to follow Christ for their whole lives—that's a choice they will each make on their own. We can't give our children a new heart, but Jesus is in the business of making hearts new. We can be faithful to introduce our kids to Jesus *and* trust him to do his work.

In the end, this book isn't about our kids. It's about *us*. It's about being confident in our calling as our kids' spiritual leaders. It's about trusting the process, trusting God, and growing along with the kids we love. Our job is to point to Christ, and this process will equip us to do that job consistently and confidently. We want to cultivate and nourish the soil of our children's hearts so they are receptive to the gospel.

Ryan Coatney from the family discipleship ministry Cross Formed Kids often says, "Raising Christian kids is always a miracle, but it's never an accident."[1] We can't make our kids be Christians, but we can give them a compelling understanding of who Jesus is and how he is relevant to their actual lives. So let's step into this process together. You're on your way to becoming the confident Christian parent you dream of being.

KEY POINTS

- We can fulfill our calling to share our faith with our families without having to know it all or do it all.

- We can grow an open, positive relationship with our children while slowly helping them weave an authentic, Christ-centered faith.

- Small but consistent choices have the power to crack into a busy routine and change the terrain of our family's faith.

- Our job is to consistently point our kids to Christ, but our kids still have to make the choice to follow.

MISTY'S STORY

I have four daughters, ages nineteen, seventeen, fourteen, and ten. It has never worked for us all to do Bible study together. However, my fourteen-year-old was open to doing a simple Bible study on the book of Mark.[2] It was a game changer. My fourteen-year-old and I took around three months about three to five nights a week and went through Mark. When we were done, she said, "What's next?" My mamma heart is happy. We are now going through John together, getting to know more of Jesus and having some great discussions. We invite the sisters, and they join in occasionally.

It all started with one night, one conversation, one tiny habit.[3]

MISTY STEINLOSKI

PART ONE

PERFECTLY

POSITIONED

FOR

GROWTH

As A KID, I loathed having to work in the family garden. To be fair, my parents didn't ask much of me, but the little I did have to do felt like agony. When I was a teen, I attempted to grow flowers on my windowsill, but after they grew spindly stems that couldn't hold the weight of a single leaf, I wrote myself off as an official Plant Killer.

Suffice it to say, no one—me included—ever expected me to become the avid gardener I am today.

What changed me from Plant Killer to Master Gardener?

In my first year of marriage, I worked in a friend's greenhouse for a season. She loved everything green, taught me how to repot seedlings and adequately water them, and eventually inspired me to bring a few tomato plants home. When I plopped the plants into pots and stuck them on the steps leading to our basement suite, I didn't expect much. But to my shock, they grew big and strong and gave us many delicious tomatoes.

From then on, I was hooked. In each consecutive rental home, my garden became a little bit bigger, until at one point, I dug up our entire front yard and turned it into a food forest. Not only had I caught the vision for gardening, but my identity had changed: I began to believe that I was capable of being a gardener.

We're going to embark on a similar journey in these pages. I love everything about family discipleship, and I want you to catch the vision for tending the hearts of the kids in your care: why it matters and why *you* are the best person for the job.

Even if you currently feel like the spiritual equivalent of a Plant Killer, you, as a parent, grandparent, or other ordinary human being, are the right person to disciple the children God has given you. You are perfectly positioned to be a Master Gardener in the hearts of children.

It's time for your identity to change.

THE POWER OF A PARENT

**Understanding the Biggest
Influence on a Child's Faith**

As I CHATTED WITH OTHER VOLUNTEERS at the orchestra fundraiser, the conversation took a surprising turn. A retired schoolteacher from a local Catholic school began talking about her experiences teaching junior high religion class. Almost out of the blue, she shared the very thing I'd been discovering myself: "Kids get their faith from their parents. Parents have the biggest influence on their kids' faith."

Of course, my ears perked up. This woman didn't have any kids of her own, but she had noticed what was happening in other families. One of the other women in the room asked a natural follow-up question: "Not their peers? It sure seems like they have a lot more influence!"

"No," the retired teacher said emphatically. "It's definitely their parents."

How does faith in Jesus get passed on? From person to

person and life to life, through word of mouth. That's how Christianity grew from a small group of persecuted people who followed a Jewish man named Yeshua—and how even today, in parts of the world where Christians are kidnapped, murdered, or chased out of the country, people still choose to follow Jesus. They see the work of Christ in the lives of their family members and neighbors, and faith gets passed on like one candle lighting another until the light brightens the whole room.

Psalm 145:4 tells us, "Let each generation tell its children of your mighty acts; let them proclaim your power." When each generation tells its children about our incredible God—about his power and love and the sacrifice of Jesus Christ—the new generation is equipped to choose to follow Jesus.

If you grew up in church, you might think I'm talking about Sunday school or other children's programming, but I'm not. In fact, Sunday school wasn't invented until the 1780s, and it was originally created to teach illiterate, working children how to read. It wasn't until the 1870s that Sunday school became a strictly religious program.[1]

Somehow, Christianity managed to thrive for nearly two thousand years without dedicated church teaching for children. How?

Families.

Grandmas and grandpas, moms and dads, aunts and uncles shared their faith with kids in everyday moments.

PARENT POWER

I worked on staff in children's ministries for about sixteen years, spending about ten of those as the director. That's when I first discovered the enormous power we parents have when investing in our kids' lifelong faith. In children's ministry, I was spending twenty hours (or more) per week on a one-hour program—and parents were with their kids for hours every single day.

A NOTE ABOUT FAMILY DISCIPLESHIP

Sometimes we think discipleship is only one parent's job. The evangelical church has historically held that the father is the spiritual leader of the home, but sometimes that teaching makes us moms feel worried that we'll step on our husband's toes if we read the Bible with our kids. Or maybe we think discipleship is only the mom's job because in many families she's the parent who spends more time with the kids.

But discipleship is the job of *every* Christian. We are all called to make disciples, and that includes making disciples of the little people in our homes! (By the way, the same is true if you're a grandparent or other significant figure in a child's life.)

We should strive to be on the same page with our spouse if possible, but if not, we need to remember that we're ultimately responsible to Christ. The best way to encourage our spouse to follow Christ is to be filled with love, joy, and peace and to let the Spirit change how we interact with our family. We're not responsible for our spouse's faith. We are only responsible for our own response to God. Be respectful, be kind, and follow God's leading.

A research project from the UK found that "a child attending a church group one hour a week would need to attend for

421 years to equal the same amount of time they would spend with a parent before the age of 10."[2] Isn't that mind-boggling? Children's ministry has value in teaching kids the Bible, but as parents, we have a much deeper ability to disciple our own kids simply because of the relationships we have with our children.

You're likely familiar with the term *disciple* as a noun. The disciples were Jesus' first followers—those men and women who lived with him, ate with him, and participated in his ministry. The verb *disciple* means to help someone follow in Jesus' footsteps. Discipleship is most effective when we do life with those we're discipling, and who does life with our children more than us?

A few decades ago, a study done by the Search Institute showed that the most significant spiritual influence in the life of a teenager was the mother.[3] The second most influential person was the father, then grandparents. Friends ranked sixth on the list, followed by pastors (seventh), Sunday school teachers (tenth), and youth leaders (thirteenth). And more recent data shows that these significant spiritual influences haven't changed much. In a 2016 Youth for Christ report, teens overwhelmingly indicated that their family had the most influence on their faith.[4]

But aren't young people leaving the church in droves? you may be thinking. A 2007 study by Lifeway Research showed a trend that continues today: "More than two-thirds of young adults who attend a Protestant church for at least a year in high school will stop attending church regularly for at least a year between the ages of 18 and 22."[5] Even in the early 2000s, only 30 percent of teens remained consistently invested in church as young adults. (Lack of church activity doesn't always mean lack of faith, but vibrant faith is usually connected to being in some sort of church community.) But that's not the end of the story. A few years later, data from the National Study of Youth and Religion (NSYR) showed this unexpected result: 82 percent of children of Christian parents who walked the walk and talked the talk, considered their beliefs very important, and participated in their congregations were active in their faith as young adults.[6]

What accounts for the difference between these studies— between the 30 percent and the 82 percent? The NSYR study looked specifically at teens with spiritually active parents, whereas the Lifeway study looked at any young person who had attended church regularly for at least a year as a teenager. That means parents play a key role in helping their kids grow a faith that sticks. Most teens who are leaving the church in droves have parents who aren't engaged in their own spiritual growth. (An important caveat, though: We should never judge a parent by their prodigal; even spiritually active parents face the grief of their kids choosing to walk away.)

The NSYR data also demonstrated that Christian families who encouraged talking about faith at home were more likely to have teens who remained faithful. Parents who felt guilty for pointing their children in a *specific* faith direction ended up having kids with *no* faith direction. There is a direct connection between a parent's willingness to talk about faith at home and a child's future faith life.

A different study published by Lifeway in 2017 describes the fifteen characteristics of children who continue to choose Christ as adults.[7] The most influential characteristics are

- reading the Bible regularly,
- praying regularly,
- serving in church regularly, and
- primarily listening to Christian music.

While peers have an impact on listening preferences and sometimes on a teen's willingness to serve in church, home life plays very heavily into all these habits. Sunday school teachers can tell kids over and over to "read your Bible every day," but unless it's a practice in the home, competing priorities tend to win. A child who reads the Bible regularly during the week likely has a parent who either modeled or directly taught that practice.

Why do parents have such influence? Because developing a child's faith isn't just about passing on correct theology or doctrinal points, and it's not about having the perfect curriculum. Faith grows inside relationships, like the ones Jesus had with his disciples, the kind that are hard to build in an hour-a-week program. In fact, a long-term research study showed that the health of family faith is directly linked with how connected kids feel to their parents.[8] The more family warmth you share—in other words, the more connected your kids feel to you—the more likely your kids are to continue on in your faith. Sharing Jesus is just as much about the relationship you're building with your kids as it is about the overtly spiritual habits you implement in your family. Because we have the greatest potential for deep relationships with our kids, we are perfectly positioned to disciple them.

PLANTING SEEDS OF FAITH

We have the privilege of sharing the gospel with the kids in our homes. The trouble is that we don't always know where to start, or if we have started, we don't know if we're doing it right. You might not have grown up with God. Or maybe, like me, you grew up with the church doing most of your faith development.

As a kid, I was in church multiple times a week for Sunday

school, girls' club, youth group, and Sunday evening church, and I'm not an outlier. Over the past few decades, churches have created a myriad of programs to help kids know God. I've heard children's ministry leaders lament that parents aren't interested in discipling their children anymore, but as a church, we're perpetuating this cycle. We pull kids from the main church service to give them a fun, age-appropriate faith education, essentially saying to parents, "Drop your kids off, and the professionals will take care of this." (The ironic part is that other than a stray staff member, nearly all the "professionals" are volunteers—either other parents or teenagers!)

Over time, we've lost the home-based faith habits that kept authentic, countercultural Christianity thriving for two millennia. Since we've entrusted our children's faith development to church ministries, we struggle to know how to be spiritual leaders in our homes—or even to realize that we should.

It's time to take back this intergenerational faith. No matter who you are, where your kids go to school, how busy you are, how long you've been following Jesus, or how many faith questions you have, you can develop the confidence to follow your calling as a spiritual leader in your home. You *can* draw near to God and bring your children in closer as well.

Yes, God does the hardest work in discipleship: saving us and helping us become more like Christ. When it comes to our kids, we might be tempted to think that faith is just between God and our child. But while God can (and does) draw people toward himself without any human intervention and our kids have the choice to follow or not, we have the privilege and the calling to actively participate in the process. We get to partner with God to cultivate the soil of our children's hearts and plant seeds of faith.

Jesus told a parable about a person sowing seeds on different kinds of ground to demonstrate how his Good News takes root (or doesn't) in our lives. He said,

> "Listen! A farmer went out to plant some seeds. As he scattered them across his field, some seeds fell on a footpath, and the birds came and ate them. Other seeds fell on shallow soil with underlying rock. The seeds sprouted quickly because the soil was shallow. But the plants soon wilted under the hot sun, and since they didn't have deep roots, they died. Other seeds fell among thorns that grew up and choked out the tender plants. Still other seeds fell on fertile soil, and they produced a crop that was thirty, sixty, and even a hundred times as much as had been planted!"
>
> MATTHEW 13:3-8

How does this parable apply to family faith? Well, you can be ready and willing to plant seeds of faith in your kids, but there are a lot of issues you might run into that stop growth from happening. Three of these soils help us understand the obstacles ahead.

Rocky Soil

The seeds that fall on rocky soil sprout quickly but don't put down roots, so when the sun comes up, these plants wither. Rocky soil is a problem because while plants can sprout and start growing, their roots can't properly tether the plant to the ground or soak up water and nutrients.

You might not immediately notice rocky soil in your family. If you started enthusiastically discipling your kids and were excited about doing all the things with them but lost heart when the emotions wore off and family faith development became tough, you've got rocky soil. In a home with rocky soil, teaching the gospel gets abandoned because it seems too hard. We don't know how to answer their questions, they won't sit still, or they're constantly turning the conversation to bathroom topics—so it's easier to wither and opt out.

Weedy Soil

Some of the seeds fall among thorny weeds, which means that as the seeds sprout, the plants get overwhelmed and choked out. Weeds steal nutrients, water, and sunlight from the plants you want to grow.

Weeds can grow at any point in your family life. You may start off discipling your kids with confidence, but then life gets busy and distracting and those weeds crowd out spiritual disciplines. Sports, homework, friends, and music practice take all your family time, and you don't know how to redeem the moments you *do* have. Teaching the gospel gets abandoned because the weeds of life have stolen your time, energy, and motivation.

Good Soil

Some of the seeds fall on good soil and produce a harvest beyond the farmer's wildest dreams. This is the kind of family faith soil we want: for the seeds of the gospel to be cast first into our own soft hearts and then to grow abundantly in our family. We don't need to do it all or know it all to have an incredible harvest. We're just the farmer, casting the seed onto good soil. The Holy Spirit is the one who makes those seeds of faith grow.

I find this truth both freeing and convicting. We can be confident that God loves our children even more than we do and is doing the hardest work of heart change. But we are called to plant the seeds. Let's face it: We all have some rocky or weedy soil in our lives. We all have times when it's not fun or easy to plant seeds of faith in our kids . . . so we just don't do it. We all have seasons when the busyness and distractions of life threaten to choke out time spent with God. This is part of being human. But that doesn't mean we don't have any good soil (or at least the potential for good soil). When we're faithful to plant seeds of faith in our hearts and families, not even rocks and weeds and times of drought can prevent a harvest.

KEY POINTS

- Parents play a key role in helping their kids grow a faith that sticks.
- Discipleship is most effective when we do life with those we're discipling, and who does life with our kids more than us?
- Faith development isn't just about passing on correct theology or doctrinal points—faith grows inside healthy relationships.
- While God can draw people toward himself without any human intervention, he calls us to partner with him in the process.
- We have a calling to plant seeds of faith, but we can be confident that God loves our children even more than we do and is doing the hardest work of heart change.

· · · · · · · · · **YOUR TURN** · · · · · · · · ·

1. What role has church played in your own faith development?

    _____

    _____

2. What role has church played in your child's faith development?

    _____

    _____

3. What are the "rocks and weeds" that keep you from planting seeds of faith?

    _____

    _____

4. What is one thing you want to remember from this chapter?

    _____

    _____

TARA'S STORY

Our family has always had flexible quiet times with God. During different seasons, that time has looked like memory verses posted in the kitchen, a devotional at breakfast, or praying in the car.

When my sons were two, five, and seven, we started speaking nightly blessings over our kids.[9] It fit well in that season because my best intentions to pray at bedtime never worked. My sons quickly adapted the nightly blessing to their own personalities. My oldest enjoyed the same blessing every night for years. My middle son changed it up every night. And my youngest turned his into a song. I love how this one holy habit fits each personality.

After we had been doing these nightly blessings for a little over a year, I had surgery on both feet, one right after the other. For weeks I had to sit in my recliner with my feet up while my mom and Grammy took care of the boys and me.

Between the pain and the prescriptions, all our regular habits fell away. We were in survival mode and down to only those things most necessary. Even though the memory verses, devotionals, and prayer time didn't happen, the blessing habit stuck. It was easy for me to do from my recliner, and since I had memorized the blessings months before, I could remember them even with painkillers in my system.

Now, five years later, nightly blessings are still our foundational holy habit. We've added back in our other habits, but even on days when we are too tired, too busy, too everything . . . this is the habit that sticks.[10]

TARA L. COLE

STRUGGLES AND SOLUTIONS

Flipping the Script on the Problems We Encounter

HAVE YOU EVER TRIED TO COPY the way another family or an influencer does family faith, only to have the attempt fall flat? Once, a friend of mine tried to start a post-dinner hymn-singing time with her family . . . while her kids were nearly all teenagers. I bet you can guess how that went over.

Eye rolls.

Groans.

A sudden, desperate need to finish a school project that wasn't due for a week.

My friend was trying to copy something she saw in another family, but it was an obvious bust.

We might like an idea or think it sounds like something a "good" Christian parent might do, but when it doesn't go the way we thought it should, we either continue making everyone (including ourselves) miserable or we quit. We're still on the all-out team: trying everything we can think of, then becoming discouraged and eventually giving up. "All or nothing" thinking usually leaves us with . . . nothing.

We already know that parents play a key role in helping their kids develop a faith that sticks, but we also know that a lot of struggles come our way. Despite our best efforts, our kids check out, goof off, or roll their eyes. Before we map out a better way, let's take a closer look at what hasn't been working and why. Sometimes our struggles are simply a matter of perspective: Just because something is hard doesn't make it "bad" or mean you're doing something wrong. But as I've surveyed and connected with parents over the years, I've discovered that a lot of us are dealing with the same struggles—and most of those can be solved by simple perspective shifts. We think we have only the two options—push forward or quit—but in most cases, there's a third option. Let's explore four common struggles I hear about from moms and dads—and how a fresh approach can help flip the script running through your head.

STRUGGLE #1: NOTHING SEEMS TO WORK FOR ME.

Maybe, like my friend, you decided it was important to sing hymns together after supper because that's what your neighbor's family does, but when you tried it, everyone gave you the stink eye and mumbled their way through the songs.

Or maybe you saw an Instagram influencer talk about these amazing Bible study workbooks all her kids are happily doing, and it made you feel like you're failing. You quickly ordered some, only to discover your kids *hate* writing down answers in those books, even if they get to use sparkly green gel pens.

What went wrong? And what's a better way?

Mistake: You're trying to copy someone else.

What they're doing is working for *their* family. Your family is unique! You have a unique schedule, your kids have unique personalities, your family has a unique faith background and heritage, and you also have a unique cultural background.

But while a unique approach *sounds* great, we feel daunted by even starting the task of figuring that out. Plus, we may be married to someone whose spiritual heritage differs from ours, which can cause conflict. So instead, why not look for ideas to people who seem to have it all together?

The thing is, copying another family means we're not paying attention to *our* family's unique needs. What works for one family's faith formation may be very different from what works for us. That's not a failure—it just means we need to flip the script. Nothing seems to work *because* we're copying and pasting someone else's answer. So how can we find our own answer?

Solution: Ask God what he wants for your family.

In the book of Judges, when God called Gideon to fight back against the Midianites, who were oppressing Israel, Gideon did the logical first thing: He blasted a trumpet, calling his family and neighbors to arms. But then God told Gideon that his army was too big; they would boast that they had won the battle instead of giving glory to God. By the time God showed Gideon how to rightsize the army, only three hundred men remained—0.2 percent of the enemy army's numbers!

Then God gave Gideon a simple strategy for using the small army in an unusual way. Gideon and his army surrounded the Midianite camp at night, smashed the jars covering their torches, let the flames leap to life, and sounded shofars. In fear, some of the Midianites turned on each other, and the rest ran away. Gideon and his tiny army routed their enemies with music and light (Judges 6–7).

Gideon took stock of his context, sought God for insights, and then used a simple strategy that harnessed the power of something small. The same principles apply to family faith formation:

1. **Take stock of the context.** What's going on in your family? What schedules and personalities are in the mix? What engages your kids? What bores them?

2. **Seek God for insights.** Is there a specific goal he's placing on your heart, like teaching your kids about worship or reading through Psalms together? You can take that goal and ask God to show you ways to do it that make sense for your unique family.

3. **Make a simple strategy that harnesses the power of something small.** The best way to find your strategy is to ask the following questions: *How can I invite God into what we're already doing? Where do I notice small pauses in our day? Where and when do we tend to gather?* If I want to introduce my kids to the Psalms, I might decide to write a few verses from a favorite psalm on the bathroom mirror, reading it to my kids when I'm brushing their teeth. My husband might read a psalm during supper as the kids are chewing.

When we invite God into the process of discipling our kids, we'll discover many ways to incorporate the Bible and prayer into our days without it feeling like a legalistic chore. We want to invite God to do his work in his way in our unique family, rather than trying to mimic what he's doing in someone else's family.

STRUGGLE #2: MY KIDS WON'T LISTEN.

Have you ever felt like pulling your hair out as you try to read the Bible or pray with your kids? Kids who *were* sitting quietly during their bedtime story suddenly need to do backflips on their bed as soon as you open a storybook Bible.

In these moments, we're tempted to force our kids to buckle down and pay attention. We get frustrated (*This is important stuff! I want them to understand!*) and afraid (*What if they don't understand God's love for them? What if they turn away from him because I couldn't get them to listen?*). We might even raise our voice to get them to pay attention so we can just read this Bible story to them already! (I've been guilty of that.)

No matter what we do, our kids just balk and complain and say, "I don't want to do this." Doesn't really get us super motivated to make it a habit, right? What's going wrong?

Mistake: You're trying to make kids sit quietly and pay attention.

When our kids stop listening, they aren't the problem; we are. We think if they're not sitting still and listening quietly, they're not paying attention or learning. But when we tell them, "Sit still, listen, and stop squirming. This is important!" we don't get engaged kids who can't wait to share their insights with us. Most kids equate sitting still with being bored! Telling our kids to "sit still and listen" is a great way to push them away from God, and maybe even from us. And the truth is, sitting still and listening quietly *does not equal* engaged learning for a lot of kids. Quiet kids are just as likely to be zoned out as they are to be engaged, and sometimes the most engaged child is the one who's running around the kitchen while you talk.

Solution: Focus on engaging your kids.

How did God get his point across to the ancient Israelites? It wasn't all sermons and prophetic messages! Multiple yearly festivals offered chances to learn through doing instead of just through listening. At the Passover feast, every food had a symbolic meaning, and kids would ask questions about the reasons for Passover as they ate. At the Feast of Booths, Israelite families built temporary shelters and slept in them for a week to remind them of their time in the desert with Moses. Israelite religious culture included regularly singing psalms, offering sacrifices, and memorizing Scriptures. Occasionally, prophets even became living object lessons.[1] God isn't limited to lectures and three-point sermons, and neither are we.

So how can we flip the script on misbehavior and instead choose to engage our kids with practical, realistic little habits?

- **Devotionals and Scripture Reading:** Devotionals and Scripture reading are times we're especially tempted to push the *sit still and listen* approach. Instead, consider what captures your kids' attention and works with their unique personalities! You'll discover everyone is a lot more engaged.
  - Create a Bible study approach that they're interested in! You can find devotionals about dinosaurs, science, or princesses, or books full of fun infographics.
  - Allow your kids to wiggle and interrupt and ask questions. You might find your "devotional time"

taking a little longer, but your kids will get a lot more out of it.

- Let your kids create art, color, or even quietly play while you read the Bible. Kids usually listen better and retain more when their hands are busy. If you're open to it, you can even act out Bible stories with them. This helps them retain facts and sequences better than simply listening.

• **Prayer:** In his book *Habits of the Household*, Justin Whitmel Earley points out, "In family, if you're adverse to messy prayers, then you're adverse to prayer."[2] To engage your kids in prayer, don't be afraid to mix things up! Help them focus on tangible things and connect the conversation with God more immediately to their lives.

- Pass around a pair of socks, inviting the child holding the socks to pray a short prayer. Having a physical item to focus on helps their brains stay more engaged and makes praying more fun. God created our children to be playful, and I believe he's delighted when we invite little ones to use that gift in prayer.
- Go for a walk outside and thank God for each thing you see.
- Invite your kids to draw or write out prayer requests.

• **Scripture Memorization:** Memorization helps kids move God's Word from their heads to their hearts as they remember his truths during everyday situations. Look for ways to make the memorization more creative and, well, memorable!

- Put actions to the verse.
- Have your kids turn the verse into a song.
- Play a Scripture memory game.

- **Worship:** Making music at church or at home is a fabulous way to help your kids connect with God, but this can be tricky if your church doesn't have a regular, recognizable repertoire of songs. Look for ways to allow your child to move (age appropriately) during worship so they can fall in love with worshiping God.
  - Offer a flag or streamers to wave. This allows wiggly and nonverbal kids to participate in worship too.
  - Talk about the purpose of worship time. Sometimes kids just need to know the *why* before they can fully engage.
  - Listen (and dance!) to the songs from church at home so your kids are familiar with them.

The *sit still and listen* approach doesn't foster growth for most kids; it usually fosters rebellion or empty obedience. If you want to step away from family discipleship that feels legalistic, don't focus on simply getting your kids to listen. Remember, sharing Jesus with our kids isn't about getting as much info into them as possible—it's about relationships. When you consider your kids' interests, allow them to wiggle and interrupt, or let them create art or even play while you're reading or praying, you're saying to your kids, "I value this, and I value *you*" rather than "I value this more than you."

STRUGGLE #3: I DON'T HAVE ENOUGH TIME.

Let's imagine I read that I should spend ten to fifteen minutes in the mornings reading the Bible and praying with my kids before they start school. My husband is at work by 7:30 a.m., so I'm hustling through everything else just to fit this plan in. Getting kids dressed and fed, loading/unloading the dishwasher, getting everyone in the car, driving to school—what could possibly be taken out? Maybe I could wake up earlier? Or deal with the dishwasher later? It feels so complicated, and I'm tired, so after a couple of days, it's easier to just let it slide.

Talking to your kids about faith or teaching the Bible to them can feel like just another item to add to your already overflowing to-do list. It's tough to remember to do something every day or to make sure it's becoming part of the routine. Plus, you're not sure you *want* it to become routine, because you don't want it to feel like a legalistic chore. Wouldn't it be easier if we just waited for conversations about faith to come up naturally?

Mistake: You've made faith part of your to-do list.

You've probably heard this analogy: The priorities of our day are like a jar of rocks, pebbles, and sand. To fit everything into the jar, we put the big rocks (*must do*) in first, then add the smaller rocks (*should do*) and sand (*fit in somehow*).

Faith *is* supposed to be one of those big rocks, right? But because our life jars are full to the brim, we think we must take something *out* to fit God *in*. And when everything else feels urgent, finding the time to consistently invest in our kids' faith formation can take a back seat because there's no room for another big rock in our jar.

Solution: Prioritize small, intentional moments to help your kids connect with God.

What if, instead of being one of those rocks, faith is the sand? In the jar illustration, the sand normally represents the low-priority tasks that we fit in when we can. But sand doesn't have to represent our lowest priorities. We can flip the metaphor around! Sand fits in all the cracks, surrounding and connecting every rock and pebble. Acts 17:28 says, "In him we live and move and exist," and Colossians 1:17 says, "He existed before anything else, and he holds all creation together." God doesn't want a relationship where he's a compartmentalized item to check off a to-do list. He's already in every part of our day. What if we decided to just help our children meet him there?

In Deuteronomy 6:6-7, Moses tells the Israelites,

> "You must commit yourselves wholeheartedly to these commands that I am giving you today. Repeat them again and again to your children. Talk about them when you are at home and when you are on the road, when you are going to bed and when you are getting up."

The families who first heard these words were *busy*—and nothing about their context made this kind of consistency easy. The Israelites were refugees, fleeing from generations of enslavement. They lived in a nomadic tent city in the desert. The women spent their days cooking, cleaning, caring for their children, and dumping sand out of every sandal (sound familiar, anyone?), and the men spent their days shepherding in the wilderness, caring for the Tabernacle, and learning to be warriors. God didn't ask the Israelites to add anything to their lives.

These parents were to talk about God and his commandments *whenever they were with their kids, whatever they were doing*: baking bread, lambing, or trekking to the next campsite.

So what does that mean for us?

When faith is the sand instead of a big rock, we intentionally build small moments into our days to help our children connect with God. In modern times, this might look like reading a short devotional at breakfast, praying a blessing over the kids when dropping them off at school, singing worship songs while bathing the toddler, or doing a prayer time while tucking each kid into bed. Approaching faith development as thirty-second moments tucked into the nooks and crannies of life (even just a couple of them) means we help our children see God not as an item on a to-do list but as part of the rhythm of our days.

This is what the bit-by-bit team discovers along the way: When we intentionally weave in these small faith moments, we'll also get spontaneous teachable moments—but those teachable moments will come a lot more naturally when we've already normalized consistently talking to God, reading the Bible, and talking about faith through our thirty-second moments.

STRUGGLE #4: I DON'T KNOW ENOUGH TO DISCIPLE MY KIDS.

Do you feel like everyone else—that homeschool mom down the road whose kids do Bible studies every morning, your child's Sunday school teacher, the Bible teacher at the Christian school—is better qualified to teach your kids about faith? We take our kids to piano teachers or soccer coaches, so shouldn't we take them to experts to teach them the Bible?

Perhaps your own faith was largely formed by the church, so doing something at home feels like learning a foreign language. Or maybe you were raised by solid Christian parents who did all the things with you, but you found it off-putting as a child and don't want the same experience for your kids. Or maybe you came to Christ as an adult and don't have the first clue how to communicate what you've discovered in kid-friendly terms.

And then there's the fear of getting things wrong. What if you mess up this discipleship thing and your kids end up feeling forced into faith, or you don't explain it well and they end up with terrible theology for life? Having our kids learn from trained people who "know more" can certainly feel safer.

Mistake: You think you need to know more.

God doesn't expect us to know enough—and that's because he wants us to rely on him. Discipling our kids (or anyone else) is not a job we're supposed to handle on our own, in our own power. In one of my favorite verses in the book of Acts, Peter and John have been brought in front of the religious leaders to be questioned about a healing they'd done. Acts 4:13 says,

> The members of the council were amazed when they
> saw the boldness of Peter and John, for they could see
> that they were ordinary men with no special training in
> the Scriptures. They also recognized them as men who
> had been with Jesus.

What changed these guys from normal dudes into powerful Christians who helped build the early church? It wasn't more education—it was Jesus. Spending time with Jesus and being filled with the Holy Spirit was enough to turn them into powerhouses. The same is true for you. You don't need to have attended Christian school, read the whole Bible, or obtained a seminary degree to be qualified. Just like with the early disciples, it's not what you know but Who you know that matters.

Let's imagine that you decide to wait to disciple your kids until you think you know enough, like maybe after you've read the whole Bible or at least a couple of theology books. How does that impact the amount of time they're exposed to faith?

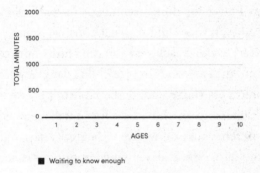

Amount of Time Spent Discipling
When We Wait to Know Enough

Waiting to know enough

If you choose to wait until you feel fully equipped, you'll spend zero time talking about God or reading the Bible during some of the most formative years of your child's life. Doing nothing out of fear that you'll get it wrong means you end up with the same results: nothing.

And if you're still feeling uncertain, here's something important to remember: Paul told the people of Corinth, "It is not that we think we are qualified to do anything on our own. Our qualification comes from God. He has enabled us to be ministers of his new covenant" (2 Corinthians 3:5-6). If Paul felt unqualified, it's no wonder we feel unqualified too.

But God worked through Paul to spread the gospel in all sorts of ways and places, and God can use you to spread the gospel effectively in your own home. But even if you still feel unqualified, there's one more way we can flip the script so you can move forward.

Solution: Start little.

What if—no matter how unqualified you feel—instead of doing nothing, you trust that God will guide you if you just start with something little? Let's imagine you start with a thirty-second faith routine when your child is a year old. You can pray the Lord's Prayer for thirty seconds or read a Bible verse out loud as you tuck your child in. That's doable, right?

Then let's say that each year you get a little more confident, and you add thirty seconds to your child's day every year. When your child is two, you're reading the Bible or praying with your child or listening to worship music for a total of one minute per day. By age ten, you're doing five minutes per day. What might be the long-term difference between letting your lack of official

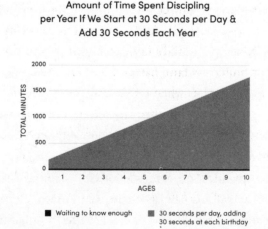

Amount of Time Spent Discipling
per Year If We Start at 30 Seconds per Day &
Add 30 Seconds Each Year

qualifications keep you frozen . . . and stepping forward with little steps, trusting God to bring the increase?

By the time your child is ten years old, you're spending nearly two thousand minutes *per year* in intentional conversations and prayer with your child. That may not sound like a lot in the grand scheme of things, but God has always used small beginnings to do great work.

Consider the Israelites: After they returned from exile in Babylon, they began rebuilding the Temple—and the neighboring nations kicked up a fuss with the king of Persia. The Israelites were scared, so for years, they let their fear keep them from rebuilding the Temple.

Finally, God spoke to a young priest, telling Zechariah that Israel needed to get back to work on the Temple. They weren't going to get it built in a night, but God said, "Do not despise these small beginnings, for the LORD rejoices to see the work begin" (Zechariah 4:10).

You may be tempted to despise small beginnings, wondering what difference this habit could possibly make in your child's life. But just as the Temple couldn't be rebuilt until the builders laid the first stone, your child's faith won't be built until you start the first small habit. And like the Temple being raised, stone by stone, your child's faith will grow as you slowly and sustainably build tiny faith habits into your life.

And what happens when those small habits add up?

When you choose to spend small, intentional moments sharing Jesus with your child, your small faith investments will gain compound interest! With just thirty seconds per day, adding an additional thirty seconds every year, you'll have spent 167 hours actively sharing Jesus with your child by the time they are ten years old.

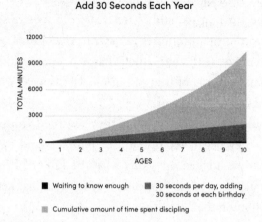

Cumulative Amount of Time Spent Discipling
If We Start at 30 Seconds per Day &
Add 30 Seconds Each Year

■ Waiting to know enough ▨ 30 seconds per day, adding
30 seconds at each birthday

▨ Cumulative amount of time spent discipling

Jesus specializes in taking our little and turning it into a lot. Remember how he took five loaves of bread and two fish and fed thousands? We don't need a lot when we bring our *little* to God.

PUTTING THE SOLUTIONS TOGETHER

How do we seek God's guidance, engage our kids, prioritize small moments, and start little—and see our family's spiritual life change in sustainable and transformative ways? In his book *Tiny Habits: The Small Changes That Change Everything*, behavioral psychologist and Stanford University professor BJ Fogg compares wanting to change your life to the desire to cultivate a garden:

> You could stand on your back porch and wish that your scraggly yard would somehow become beautiful. As the weeks go by, weeds begin to grow. You pull a few out here and there, but this becomes laborious so you stop. But you keep wishing that beautiful things would grow instead.[3]

I used to feel overwhelmed as I looked at everyone else's beautiful, curated, flourishing family garden—because my family garden looked nothing like theirs. I made every mistake we've talked about in this chapter! But as I prayed over my struggles, I realized that Fogg's observation is also true of family discipleship. I decided to invest in my children's spiritual growth through the power of starting small with simple habits. I began to create a simple process that would establish family rhythms of faith and equip my kids to grow a faith of their own. I call it the Faith Growth Cycle.

The Faith Growth Cycle identifies three stages that you can notice, pursue, and apply to all sorts of situations, personalities, and life seasons:

1. the Seed Stage,
2. the Sprout Stage, and
3. the Root Stage.

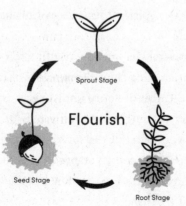

To know which specific, sustainable steps to take each time God wants to lead you or your family deeper into relationship with him, follow the Faith Growth Cycle. These three steps form a super simple plan that even exhausted parents can implement, helping your family flourish in faith without you needing to know it all or do it all. That's because the Faith Growth Cycle isn't about *what* to do at home but about *how* to do it. You'll be able to determine attainable, life-giving daily habits God wants your family to have and how to make them a reality. The best part is that you can use the cycle to flourish spiritually in any season of life. Whether you're in the toddler-tantrum or teen-taxi stage, the Faith Growth Cycle works.

Our family and many others have found this path game-changing. Small habits we began have steadily grown into reflexes and rhythms over time, leading to flourishing faith in our whole family. Would you believe my kids have started telling *me* when it is time to read the Bible together? One of my boys always reminds me that no matter how late it is, we should always read the Bible before bed. (That might be more accurately classified as a spiritual procrastination habit, but at this point, it works.)

In the next several chapters, we're going to explore clear but flexible steps for creating flourishing habits of faith. Each time God wants to lead you or your family deeper into relationship with him, understanding where you are in the Faith Growth Cycle can help you map out the specific, sustainable steps that will get you there. And as you partner with God using the Faith Growth Cycle, you'll find yourself increasingly moving into family faith that flourishes.

• • • • • • • • • KEY POINTS • • • • • • • •

- *Struggle #1: Nothing seems to work for me.*

  - *Mistake:* You're trying to copy someone else.

  - *Solution:* Ask God what he wants for your family.

  - *Key:* Discover your own strategy instead of copying and pasting someone else's.

- *Struggle #2: My kids won't listen.*

  - *Mistake:* You're trying to make kids sit quietly and pay attention.

  - *Solution*: Focus on engaging your kids.

  - *Key*: Sharing Jesus with our kids isn't about getting as much info into them as possible— it's about relationships.

- *Struggle #3: I don't have enough time.*

  - *Mistake*: You've made faith part of your to-do list.

  - *Solution*: Prioritize small, intentional moments to help your kids connect with God.

  - *Key*: Faith isn't a big rock. It's the sand that holds everything together.

- *Struggle #4: I don't know enough to disciple my kids.*

  - *Mistake*: You think you need to know more.

  - *Solution*: Start little.

  - *Key*: We don't need a lot when we bring our *little* to God.

- To know which specific, sustainable steps to take each time God wants to lead you or your family deeper into relationship with him, follow the Faith Growth Cycle.

· · · · · · · · YOUR TURN · · · · · · · · ·

1. Which of the four struggles mentioned resonates the most with you?

   _____

   _____

2. Which mistakes do you find yourself prone to making? (Personally, I've made all four mistakes, sometimes in the same day!)

   _____

   _____

3. Which solution helps you feel the most hopeful about establishing rhythms of faith in your home without forcing or pushing your kids into it?

   _____

   _____

4. What is one thing you want to remember from this chapter?

   _____

   _____

NATHANIEL'S STORY

Our approach to health and fitness has influenced our philosophy around spiritual practices:

- "Do what you will do." Or, put another way: Find what you enjoy doing. Don't force yourself into an activity you don't like.
- Make it fit your lifestyle and schedule; otherwise, it isn't sustainable.

How do these principles apply to "spiritual fitness"? Instead of feeling shame that your spiritual practices don't look a certain way, find the practices you enjoy and make them fit your lifestyle.

With my oldest daughter, we've started reading one chapter from the Gospels most days and sharing our top takeaways at bedtime. We give ourselves grace for days we are busy or not feeling well, so there is no guilt over missed days. In a week we end up with three to five days where we have discussed our thoughts about the teachings of Jesus.

We both really treasure this time, which allows us to share our faith and walk together. My daughter also commented on how she's started sleeping better: Her anxiety has lessened, and her nightmares have disappeared.[4]

NATHANIEL PETERS

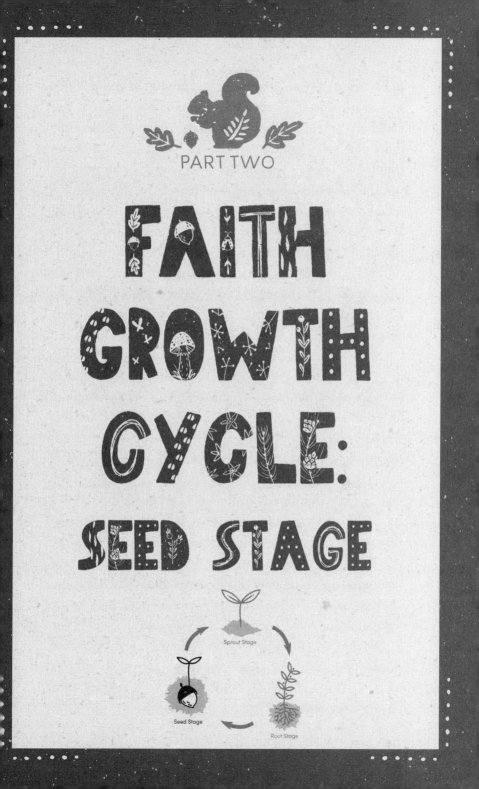

PART TWO

FAITH GROWTH CYCLE: SEED STAGE

IF I WANT TO START A GARDEN, I first need to design it: find a spot in my yard that gets enough sun and rain, cultivate and enrich the soil, pick out plants that interest me, and make sure those plants can grow in my area. If you live in a different country, I can't call you up, ask what seed varieties work for you, and expect them to grow the same way for me. Seeds that need hot weather for months won't grow properly where I live. If I want my garden to grow, I need to consult a guide to what thrives in *my* area.

This is how the Seed Stage works. If we want to help our kids grow in faith and get to know God and learn to live in the power of the Holy Spirit, we first must consult our Guide to discern what's going to grow well in our family.

In the Seed Stage, we consciously choose to let God lead us as we dig into what the Bible says about sharing our faith with our kids and with others. We choose to take our focus off our fears and instead gaze on Jesus, "the champion who initiates and perfects our faith" (Hebrews 12:2). The author of Hebrews compares the life of faith to a race and invites Christ followers to "strip off every weight that slows us down, especially the sin that so easily trips us up" (Hebrews 12:1). That's exactly what we need to do in the Seed Stage. First, we fix our eyes on Jesus, then we strip off the excuses and obstacles holding us back. We talk honestly with him about why we're here and what's been holding us back—or, if we already have some faith-filled habits at home, we ask God to show us where we might be trying to force someone else's plan onto our unique family.

We can't skip this step! Any flourishing discipleship process starts with inviting the Holy Spirit into what we do and how we do it. We can only help our kids grow in faith if we're following God's lead.

3

WHAT'S MY WHY?

Discovering Your Vision for Family Discipleship

I SIT ON THE FLOOR OF THE BATHROOM, weighed down by guilt. I have just read a blogger's lovely account of her children who happily work through their Bible studies at the table each morning. My imagination runs through the scene: her kids eagerly grabbing Bibles off the shelf, pulling freshly sharpened pencils from behind their neatly scrubbed ears, then gleefully reading, writing, and applying the Bible to their own lives.

That's not exactly how the author of the article described her experience, but it's how it plays out in my head. And in that internal replay, I feel the whisperings of the enemy.

"You're not doing enough."

"You're a bad mom."

"You never taught your kids to use workbook-style Bible studies, and now they're going to end up heathens for life."

The tangled mess of lies inside my head has revealed some

of my less-than-holy motivations for discipling my kids. Do I do it because I feel like I have to prove that I am a good mom? Or maybe I do it because I am afraid my kids will reject God otherwise?

The Seed Stage of the Faith Growth Cycle starts by making us think about our personal reasons for discipling our kids. If we don't have a vision for where we're going, we'll get stuck in comparison, insecurity, or exhaustion. Without a vision, we'll want to give up when our kids ask tough questions, yell when they're driving us bonkers, or quit when life has us so exhausted and discouraged that sharing our faith with our kids feels like one more burden being laid on us. If we're going to help our kids toward a faith that lasts, our Seed Stage has to start with a foundation of *why*.

Why am I planting those seeds in the first place?

Why do I even care about sharing Jesus with my kids?

Why should I tell the next generation of God's mighty acts?

You might think that the answer seems obvious: *I want my kids to know God.* But when I asked some other moms these questions, their answers had a secondary, underlying theme:

- "I'm afraid that my kids will grow into adults who can't think critically and can't answer questions about what they believe."
- "I'm afraid my child will choose a path that will break my heart."
- "I'm afraid they won't choose Christ."
- "I'm afraid of the bad things that my kids could get into without a solid moral foundation."
- "I'm afraid that my kids will rebel. I'm afraid that the world will snatch away my precious children and turn them into hedonistic, selfish little monsters."

That's a lot of fear! Kind of makes you want to hide inside a pillow fort, right? Is that the kind of *why* that builds a lasting faith?

Our *why* needs to be what keeps us going when the going gets rough. We need to be able to trust God with the details because we trust where he's taking us. Trust is the opposite of fear.

With that in mind, let's pause for a minute on why there seems to be so much fear involved in discipling our kids, and why this is a problem. We need to understand what pushes us toward that *why*—so that we can instead surrender that fear to God and let him lead us into a better way.

THE LIMITATIONS OF FEAR

A thirty-five-year study following multiple generations of the same twenty-five families found that a key factor in children permanently walking away from their parents' faith was "excessive or intrusive" efforts to get those children to believe:

> When highly religious parents pushed their resistant
> children to participate in religious activities . . . or to
> conform to church doctrine or moral dictates, this
> was experienced by some children as having religion
> "shoved down my throat." The result was religious
> rebellion.[1]

I've never met a parent who intended to shove religion down their child's throat. But when our kids are resistant about going to church or believing specific doctrines, fear can take over. In *Mothering by the Book*, Jennifer Pepito points out that "when fear drives our decisions, we create an atmosphere that invites opposition. It's as though we are putting up a green light for the devil to come and harass us."[2] When we allow our fear for our kids to control our actions, we're more likely to shoot down questions, lecture away doubts, force kids to come to church, and push them to conform outwardly. We do these things because we're desperate to get faith to stick, but they put us on the fast track to driving our children away from God.

I have absolutely been guilty of giving in to fear. One afternoon, I wanted my kids to watch an episode of *The Chosen* with me, and one of my boys wasn't interested. My brain went into overdrive: *What if he never connects with Jesus? What if he misses who Jesus is because he isn't seeing him portrayed vividly like in this show?* Yes, it's absurd for me to think that the only way my son will ever connect with Jesus is through a TV show. But I gave in to the fear in my heart, and I forced my son to watch with us.

Fear creates a rigid and controlling environment, which leaves little room for kids to learn to grow an actual, trusting relationship with the God who has always welcomed questions and doubts, who allows us to make mistakes, and who waits with grace-filled arms when we turn back to him. God does not want us living in fear for our children's spiritual lives. In fact, his perfect love wants to cast out fear—even the very valid fear that our children will reject the gospel:

We know how much God loves us, and we have put our trust in his love.

God is love, and all who live in love live in God, and God lives in them. And as we live in God, our love grows more perfect. So we will not be afraid on the day of judgment, but we can face him with confidence because we live like Jesus here in this world.

Such love has no fear, because perfect love expels
all fear. If we are afraid, it is for fear of punishment,
and this shows that we have not fully experienced his
perfect love.

1 JOHN 4:16-18

We are not here to scare our children into heaven or to parent
out of deep-seated fears that they will turn into prodigals or be
taken captive by worldly living. As 2 Timothy 1:7 says, "God has
not given us a spirit of fear and timidity, but of power, love, and
self-discipline." We can be bold, loving, and intentional with our
child's faith journey when we let God lead the way instead of fear.

A VISION THAT LASTS

If fear isn't a *why* that will sustain us through every season of
our family's discipleship, what is? The book of Acts shows us
the answer.

When we turn to Acts 2, we discover that after Jesus ascended
to heaven and poured out his Spirit on his followers, these men
and women suddenly became fearless. Peter, who had denied
Jesus just a couple of months before, led an impromptu Holy
Spirit–fueled revival on Pentecost. Then in Acts 3, Peter and
John healed a man who was unable to walk and dared to say it
was because of Jesus. In Acts 4, the priests and Sadducees had
them arrested, telling the disciples to stop teaching in the name
of Jesus before letting them go free.

Why were the religious leaders so insistent on forcing the
followers of Jesus into silence? Fear. Fear of the ruling authori-
ties, of losing their privileges, of losing control.

The Jews were an oppressed people with very little self-
governance, and the religious leaders were terrified of having

their few freedoms taken away. When Jesus came along, making bold statements about a new Kingdom, they tried desperately to shush him. Then the disciples continued proclaiming Jesus as King and the Son of God, and the leaders had no idea what to do with these miracle-working, loud-preaching, fearless disciples:

"What should we do with these men?" the religious leaders asked each other. "We can't deny that they have performed a miraculous sign, and everybody in Jerusalem knows about it. But to keep them from spreading their propaganda any further, we must warn them not to speak to anyone in Jesus' name again" (Acts 4:16-17).

Do you see the fear? They were afraid of the pagan culture of their conquerors, the Romans. They were afraid of losing their families and young people. They were afraid of being on the wrong end of a very sharp stick. Their fear, which they thought was protecting their culture and faith, ended up blinding them to what God was doing.

The disciples, though, saw clearly. Empowered by the Spirit, they lived in a deep faith that bypassed fear—despite facing imprisonment, persecution, and even death. And in Acts 20, we see what can truly sustain us through any season and trial: the power of a fearless, Spirit-given vision.

The apostle Paul knew God wanted him to go to Jerusalem—even as everyone around him warned him that he'd end up in jail there. But Paul didn't shrink back. God was calling him forward. Paul looked fear in the eye and said,

"I am bound by the Spirit to go to Jerusalem. I don't know what awaits me, except that the Holy Spirit tells me in city after city that jail and suffering lie ahead.

But my life is worth nothing to me unless I use it for
finishing the work assigned me by the Lord Jesus—
the work of telling others the Good News about the
wonderful grace of God."

ACTS 20:22-24

Vision propelled Paul toward wherever God called him—
a vision that looked fear in the eye and said, "You may be great,
but my God is greater."

These two different responses in Acts show us two ways we
can intentionally disciple our kids:

1. We can look at the world and see all the ways our children could be pulled away from God: addictions, mental
   illness, sexual-identity issues, secular humanism, the
   hypersexualization of society. We can look at the darkness of the world and try to shield our kids from all
   these things. We can avoid talking with them about the
   issues our culture is dealing with, then teach them only
   to defend: their faith, their lifestyle, their opinions.

Or . . .

2. We can live like the disciples did. Amid both secular
   and religiously legalistic cultures, they openly engaged
   with people in their world without letting the world distract them from their calling to lead people into something better. We, too, can live within the darkness and
   harm of the world and not let any of it distract us from
   what God is calling us to. How this plays out in your
   life will be unique to you. Maybe walking away from

fear means you unashamedly send your kids to public school . . . or maybe it means you start homeschooling. Maybe fear has been playing into your decision to not become long-term missionaries, or maybe it's guiding your choices around tech time in your home. We can guide our family into fearless faith that doesn't avoid the brokenness around us but helps us love others with godly confidence. We can also release the need to micromanage our children's faith because we have confidence in God's love and faithfulness toward our children.

Remember Jesus' parable of the mustard seed (Matthew 13:31-32)? A mustard seed starts out itty-bitty and then grows into something huge. I used to picture an enormous tree because I'm used to sky-high poplars and oaks. But did you know that mustard is a bush? It can grow into a big bush (a "tree" in comparison with other plants in the arid climate of Judea), but it's practically a weed: growing furtively and persistently, yet never dominating the whole environment. When I discovered that, I realized Jesus may have been sharing a truth about the Kingdom different from what we typically assume. This story "warns against the ultimate vulgarity of confusing size with significance."[3]

Many of us Christians in the West find ourselves in panic mode when we think our rights are at stake. But if Christ is any example, we are not supposed to fight for our rights. We are not even supposed to be dominant. We are supposed to be mustard seeds, furtively sowing peace and joy, growing the Kingdom of God in our world.

For me, discipling my children isn't about ensuring that they can defend their beliefs and stay in a safe Christian bubble, or even that they're going to make good choices. No—discipling my children means I plant little mustard seeds of truth and trust that God is softening the soil of their hearts and growing those seeds into an amazing harvest. After all, God loves my babies more than I ever could, and he is also planting seeds . . . some that I might never even know about. So with fear kicked out of the driver's seat, I can point my kids to a great God who can do great things in their lives—and let God guide my family into being Kingdom people in a world that needs hope.

YOUR PERSONAL VISION

Okay, you might be thinking, *I'm on board with kicking fear out of the driver's seat. But how do I figure out this vision part? How do I find my* why? Coming up with a vision statement sounds like something that belongs in a high-level marketing meeting, but once you set aside the fear-based motives, you'll be more likely to notice the vision God has for your family.

There's no one right way to create a vision for your family's discipleship, but some general principles can help you get started:

1. Ask God to settle your heart. If you're noticing fear still seizing control, ask God to help you trust his work in your children's hearts.

2. Spend time with God's words in Scripture. The Bible is full of passages about God's heart for his people, his relationship with us, who he wants us to be, and how he wants us to share the Good News. Some passages to consider:

You must love the LORD your God with all your
heart, all your soul, and all your strength. And
you must commit yourselves wholeheartedly
to these commands that I am giving you today.
Repeat them again and again to your children.
Talk about them when you are at home and
when you are on the road, when you are going
to bed and when you are getting up.

DEUTERONOMY 6:5-7

You are the light of the world—like a city on a
hilltop that cannot be hidden. No one lights a
lamp and then puts it under a basket. Instead,
a lamp is placed on a stand, where it gives light
to everyone in the house. In the same way, let
your good deeds shine out for all to see, so that
everyone will praise your heavenly Father.

MATTHEW 5:14-16

Go and make disciples of all the nations,
baptizing them in the name of the Father and
the Son and the Holy Spirit. Teach these new
disciples to obey all the commands I have given
you. And be sure of this: I am with you always,
even to the end of the age.

MATTHEW 28:19-20

Remain in me, and I will remain in you. For a
branch cannot produce fruit if it is severed from
the vine, and you cannot be fruitful unless you
remain in me.

JOHN 15:4

This is the way to have eternal life—to know you, the only true God, and Jesus Christ, the one you sent to earth.

JOHN 17:3

We have not stopped praying for you since we first heard about you. We ask God to give you complete knowledge of his will and to give you spiritual wisdom and understanding. Then the way you live will always honor and please the Lord, and your lives will produce every kind of good fruit. All the while, you will grow as you learn to know God better and better.

COLOSSIANS 1:9-10

Other passages to pilfer ideas from: Deuteronomy 4:9; Psalm 78:1-7; Matthew 7:24-27; John 17:20-23; Ephesians 6:1-4

As you read and reflect on the verses and passages God draws you to study, think about these four questions:

    a. Why is it important to share Jesus with others?

    b. Who is responsible for sharing Jesus with my children?

    c. Why do I think God designed it this way?

    d. What motivates me to share Jesus with my kids? Why do I do it?

3. Using your answers to these questions, write your vision statement. You can use quotes straight out of the Bible if something you read resonates. If you think in pictures rather than words, you can also create an image-based vision.

4. Don't stress about the wording or feel pressure to get your vision statement perfect. That may keep you from finishing it! Remember that *done* is better than *perfect*, every time. Your vision statement will be a living document, meant to help you focus on what God has called you to but available to revisit and adjust as you need.

5. Remember that as you and your family grow and change, your vision will probably change. Anytime you notice that the vision no longer feels like it quite fits your family, go back to God in prayer and in his Word and ask what he wants for you in this season.

6. Keep your vision somewhere where you'll be able to reflect on it often. You may want to hang it on your wall, put a sticky note on your mirror, or simply set it as the background on your computer screen.

Your vision could be as simple as the one hanging on the back wall of my church: "Knowing Christ and sharing him with others." Maybe your vision is that your kids learn to trust in God's unconditional love for them, or that they turn to God in prayer. Or perhaps your vision is for your kids to deeply understand theology or be shining lights in a dark world.

My Vision

I want my kids to experience the love of God in their lives so that they can love God, be saved by the death and resurrection of Christ, and live empowered by the Holy Spirit. I want them to have true encoun-

ters with the living God so that they can live in
their identity and calling as children of God, have
complete confidence in his love for them, and live
a life that consistently and creatively reflects Christ
in a way that is unique to who he created each of
them to be.

Your Vision

_____

_____

_____

_____

_____

_____

· · · · · · · · · KEY POINTS · · · · · · · ·

- If we make fear our reason for sharing Jesus with our kids, we'll be more likely to do the kinds of things that make kids turn away from faith.

- God does not want us living in fear for our children's spiritual lives.

- We can live with a vision like Paul's: a vision that looks fear in the eye and says, "You may be great, but my God is greater."

- God loves our kids more than we ever could and is planting seeds we might never even know about.

· · · · · · · · · **YOUR TURN** · · · · · · · ·

1. How do you think fear influenced the way you were raised?

    _____

    _____

2. Where have you seen fear influence your own parenting?

    _____

    _____

3. Can you think of other reasons to disciple kids that don't resonate with you?

    _____

    _____

4. What is one thing you want to remember from this chapter?

    _____

    _____

SARAH'S STORY

When I started learning about the Faith Growth Cycle,[4] I was struck by a comment that sometimes our faith can be based in fear. This realization was transformative for me! I realized that my faith *had* been rooted in fear. Because of fear, I had been unable to realize the true freedom that comes from the cross and the gift that Jesus gave to me.

I also realized that I may have passed this fear down into my children's faith journey. Fear has often been my default in life, and I have come to realize that it has guided my parenting, too. God revealed his truth to me in that moment.

I am now parenting differently because I am living out of God's perfect love for me. Knowing I am loved makes it easier to pass along his true and perfect love for my kids.[5]

SARAH ARMSTRONG

WHAT'S GETTING IN MY WAY?

Learning to Name and Overcome Obstacles

A FEW YEARS AGO, I desperately wanted to develop a habit of doing family devotions at the breakfast table, but I found myself faced with several obstacles:

- I ended up occupied with other things during breakfast. After dinner I often couldn't muster the energy to do the dishes and clean up the kitchen, so I would leave those things until morning. The few minutes of the day when my busy boys were all quietly(ish) eating breakfast were perfect for unloading the dishwasher and sweeping the floor.

- I couldn't find anything that met the spiritual needs of all three of my children.

- I forgot to do it.

What obstacles are currently keeping you from your calling to share Jesus with your kids? Maybe you already have some solid rhythms of faith in your family, but I bet you've still run into moments when you wanted to pick up the Bible and read with your kids and didn't, or you wanted to pray but something happened in your schedule (or heart), and it just didn't work out.

As we consider how to discern and prepare for our family's discipleship in the Seed Stage, it's important to fix our eyes on Jesus and start with our *why*. But there's another key piece we need to take to God to figure out as well: our obstacles. We need to "throw off everything that hinders [us]" from stepping into our calling (Hebrews 12:1, NIV).

We may have the strongest motivation in the world, but motivation on its own isn't enough. Everyone faces obstacles that keep them from doing what God has asked them to do.

What is holding you back? A lack of time? Motivation? Maybe your kids have diverse needs or ages, or you are facing struggles that drain you physically or emotionally.

Some of these things are within our control, and others aren't. Before we can plant seeds with the intentionality and sustainability we want, we must work with God to get our barriers out in the open so we can create space for the vision he's given us. We need to learn to either overcome or work within our limitations.

STEP #1: PRAY.

The Seed Stage should be saturated with prayer. Before you do anything else, pray over this process. Invite God in. Let him speak to you about your habits and lifestyle—and the state of your relationship with him.

God, I am almost scared to start this section because I know I'm going to be bumping up against my own sinfulness. Some of my obstacles are out of my control, but others come from inside me. Please help me be honest with myself and with you. Give me wisdom to know the difference between problems that you want me to overcome and others that I'll always need your help with. Speak to me about my habits, my lifestyle, and the state of my relationship with you. I invite you to do your work in my heart. In Jesus' name, amen.

STEP #2: LIST YOUR OBSTACLES.

When I was six, I broke my parents' rule about playing at our local pond after school. To cover it up, I told my parents I had been waiting with a friend for her bus. When my mom caught me in the lie, I locked myself in the bathroom, hoping I could hide from my punishment.

Sometimes we try to hide from ourselves, too. We tell ourselves lies that start to feel like truth and hide problems behind closed doors in our hearts until we forget they ever existed. But Psalm 139 reminds us that we can't hide from God:

I can never escape from your Spirit!
    I can never get away from your presence!
If I go up to heaven, you are there;
    if I go down to the grave, you are there.
If I ride the wings of the morning,
    if I dwell by the farthest oceans,
even there your hand will guide me,
    and your strength will support me.
I could ask the darkness to hide me
    and the light around me to become night—

> but even in darkness I cannot hide from you.
> To you the night shines as bright as day.
> Darkness and light are the same to you.

PSALM 139:7-12

We may want to hide from our obstacles or pretend they don't exist, but God already knows what they are. A beautiful thing about God is that when we genuinely and vulnerably ask him to shine as bright as day on the things we try to hide in the dark, he'll do it with gentleness. As he reveals what's going on in our hearts, we can trust him to guide us into true change.

Of course, no one likes to acknowledge their struggles, so I'll go first. Here's a full list of things I've either said or heard regarding why family discipleship feels impossible. Feel free to circle the ones that most apply to you or add to the list.

I don't have enough time in the day.

I'm too busy.

I get distracted each time I try.

I don't know how to connect with my kids spiritually.

I don't know how to answer their questions.

I feel like a hypocrite.

I never had this way of life modeled to me.

There are too many ideas. I don't know where to start.

My kids are too young for a real conversation.

My kids are too squirmy—they won't listen.

My spouse doesn't help.

My spouse doesn't approve.

My kids are bored and distracted when we do anything related to God.

I feel like I'm lecturing my child when I talk about God.

I feel like I'm forcing my faith on my child instead of
     letting them develop their own relationship with God.
My kids are too little; they won't get it.
My kids are too big and won't want to do this.
My kids are too loud or argumentative for a real conversation.
My kids always make the conversation turn into silliness.
I'm getting started too late in my kids' lives. It probably
     wouldn't even make a difference at this point.
I'm overwhelmed by life.
We don't have time in the morning/at supper/at bedtime.
I don't know enough about the Bible to teach my kids.
I don't feel like my own faith is strong enough.

From grandparents:
I'm not with my grandkids often enough.
I don't want to step on my child's toes by sharing my faith
     with their kids.

If you have kids with special needs, are parenting solo or with mental-health struggles, or are grieving a deep loss, those aren't obstacles that will change with a simple prayer and some shifts in your thinking, and neither are they sins to confess. If you find yourself with severe limitations, please know that God is always with you and that he can work through those situations.

STEP #3: CONFESS.

Philippians 1:6 says, "I am certain that God, who began the good work within you, will continue his work until it is finally finished on the day when Christ Jesus returns." Our child's faith journey is God's work. He wants our efforts to disciple them to succeed! But first we must be willing to surrender our obstacles, trusting that he can and will make a way. Exodus 34:14 says that God wants us to worship him above all others—and that includes our schedules, our priorities, our struggles, and our excuses. (Ouch. I need to remind myself of that daily.)

That's why, once you've spent time with God, asking him to reveal what's holding you back, it's time to lay those obstacles before him. When it comes to the barriers that are out of your control, bringing them before God is an acknowledgment that they are under *God's* control. He can show you a way to pursue his calling despite (and often because of) your limitations.

Lord, I look at this list of obstacles and excuses, and I cringe inside. I confess that I have put my schedule, my kids, my spouse ahead of obedience to you. I lay these obstacles down. Thank you for your forgiveness and grace. I accept both and choose to move forward in faith that you will carry this good work to completion. In Jesus' name, amen.

STEP #4: SPEAK TRUTH.

Trying to overcome our obstacles on our own is like getting a single chair and trying to use it to scale a great big wall. It just doesn't work. But God gives us an extendable ladder that can get us over any wall: his truth, revealed through his Word and the Spirit.

When an obstacle feels insurmountable, we need to reference his truth and preach it to ourselves. As we allow God's truths to permeate our hearts, our perspective shifts and our attitude changes. God enables us to climb over the wall of obstacles one rung of truth at a time.

A common hurdle I hear is "My spouse isn't interested in spiritual leadership." And the problem *seems* to be our spouses, right? In our family, I'm the one who intentionally disciples our kids, partly because it's my natural tendency and gifting, and partly because my husband wasn't sure where his own faith stood for many years. For a long time, I saw only obstacles in that reality. I felt less equipped than my husband, who grew up in a Christian school. I felt guilty because we forgot to do our family Bible study for most of the summer and my husband didn't even notice. I let discouragement drag me down when it seemed like I was doing the work alone.

It took me a long time to accept that God had given me this passion and gifting for a reason. When I eventually stopped pushing, God began to speak truth to my heart.

When I felt inadequate, God reminded me that when the little boy brought his five loaves and two fish to Jesus (John 6:1-13), Jesus turned his tiny offering into a meal for over five thousand people. When I felt like I wasn't doing enough, God reminded me that he was constantly doing the unseen work inside my children, replacing their hearts of stone with soft hearts (Ezekiel 36:26). When I felt like I was discipling alone, God reminded me of the ultimate partnership: *He* is the one who started this good work and has promised to carry it to completion (Philippians 1:6).

As I chose to listen to God's truth, he led me to a deeper realization: The problem was not with my spouse but inside my own heart. I needed to stop trying to take over the Holy Spirit's role in my husband's life; my only calling was to follow God's leading. The Bible shows us that God can use a wife's consistent faithfulness to influence her husband (1 Corinthians 7:13-16; 1 Peter 3:1-2), but we can't force that outcome. The results are up to God. Focusing on God's truth can put this difficulty—and any other we might face—in proper perspective.

- **When time is the problem:** When you say things like "I don't have enough time," "I'm too busy," or "My schedule is overwhelming," use these Scriptures to speak truth over your situation:

  Deuteronomy 4:9   Zechariah 4:10
  Deuteronomy 6:5-7   Matthew 6:33
  Psalm 78:1-7   Matthew 7:24-27
  Proverbs 22:6   John 15:4
  Ecclesiastes 3:1-8

- **When your kids are the problem:** When you're frustrated with the way your kids are responding, use these Scriptures to speak truth over your situation:

  Proverbs 15:1   Ephesians 6:4
  Matthew 18:20   Colossians 3:12
  Mark 9:36-37   1 Peter 3:15-16
  Ephesians 4:2

- **When your spouse is the problem:** When you're frustrated because your spouse doesn't seem interested in discipling your kids, use these Scriptures to speak truth over your situation:

  1 Corinthians 7:13-16   1 Peter 3:1-2

- **When you are the problem:** When you're feeling unequipped or like your own faith isn't strong enough, when your kids ask questions you don't know how to answer, or when you just keep getting distracted, use these verses to speak truth to yourself:

  Proverbs 3:5-6   2 Corinthians 3:5-6
  Isaiah 61:11   Philippians 1:6
  Matthew 6:34   Philippians 4:13
  John 6:1-13   Colossians 1:9-10
  Acts 4:13   Hebrews 4:16

STEP #5: PRAY A PRAYER OF RELEASE.

We can't create a family culture of faith simply by articulating our *why* and naming our obstacles. Ultimately, discipling our kids is never about us and what we can teach in our own strength; it's about God and his strength. Our children belong to him, and if they choose to follow him, that relationship is between him and them, not him and us. As we jump over our hurdles, we can acknowledge this reality by offering a prayer of release:

God, you are the maker of all creation, you are the maker of my family, and you are the lover of our souls. You are holy and just and have called us according to your purpose. Thank you for inviting us into relationship with you. Give us the desire for more of you each day!

You have promised that I can approach your throne of grace with confidence, so that I may receive mercy and find grace to help in my time of need. My time of need is now, and I desperately need your help. Help me trust in you with all my heart and lean not on my own understanding when it comes to spiritually parenting my children.

I am confident that you are the one who started this good work in my family, and you are the one who will carry it to completion until the day of Christ Jesus. This is all for your glory, not mine. I am confident that you equip the called, and as I am called to spiritually parent my children, I will be able to do all this through you, the one who gives me strength.

Help me remember that as garden soil causes seeds to grow, you are the one who will ultimately make righteousness and praise spring up in my family. In the power of your holy name, I claim your promise that my children will grow up to be called oaks of righteousness. May our family grow in righteousness and be part of your family forever. May we be the work of your hands for the display of your splendor. May my children be a planting of the Lord that brings honor and glory to your name. In your powerful, perfect, and holy name, amen.*

STEP #6: COMMIT.

When we've learned something, writing it on paper helps us remember it and makes it feel more concrete. So now that we have named, confessed, and released our barriers to God, we cement our work with a written pledge! Feel free to write your own to capture what you are laying before God, or use the template here (if you're feeling particularly bold, snap a picture of it and share on social media with the hashtag #littlehabitsbigfaith):

I, _____, know that I do not have to be perfect to point my children to Christ. He is the only perfect one.

I, _____, acknowledge that I don't have it all together now, and I never will. But I know the one who does, and I trust him to help me overcome all obstacles.

I, _____, am ready to follow God's call on my life and to obey his call to disciple my children.

Signature: _____

Date: _____

---

* Scriptures used to write this prayer: Proverbs 3:5-6; Isaiah 60:21, 61:3, 11; Philippians 1:6, 4:13; and Hebrews 4:16.

Tim Keller once said that "helplessness, not holiness, is the first step to accessing the presence of God."[1] We sign this pledge not because we have it all together but because we don't. If you're feeling a little helpless right now because of the obstacles you're facing, you're in the right place. Allow God to speak his peace and love and joy over you. When God is for us, what can be against us (Romans 8:31)?

· · · · · · · · KEY POINTS · · · · · · · · ·

- We may not want to acknowledge our obstacles, but God already knows what they are.
- God wants this to succeed because he wants to use you in your child's life. This is his work.
- As we allow God's truths to permeate our hearts, God enables us to climb over the wall of obstacles one rung of truth at a time.
- We are not to take over the Holy Spirit's role but to faithfully follow God.

· · · · · · · · YOUR TURN · · · · · · · · ·

1. Which of your hurdles aren't under your control? What is God saying to you about them?

    _____

    _____

2. Which of your obstacles might actually be excuses? What is God saying to you about them?

    _____

    _____

3. Look up one of the suggested verses for a barrier you're facing, and write it out here:

    _____

    _____

4. What is one thing you want to remember from this chapter?

    _____

    _____

NATALIA'S STORY

I wanted to teach my kids to love books because I want them to love the Bible, and the Bible is something we need to read. I have kids on the autism spectrum and the Bible was too difficult when they were little, so I started looking for books. I took them to libraries to check out lots of books, and we also created our own social stories together, which is something we learned from my son's therapist. The social stories made a big difference in his anxiety. I saw the power those stories had, so I started looking for Christian books to buy or ask the library to buy.

The books helped me teach my kids about God, about who he is, what their identity is. Picture books have so many visuals to help my kids grasp and make the truths their own. Reading together has given us moments not only to talk about God but also to connect with each other deeply. The other day my son was talking about God and a specific story in the Bible, and I know he learned that because of those moments I've read to him at nighttime.

Committing to this rhythm has not been easy for me. I'm not perfect at doing it every night, I've gone through various personal struggles, and sometimes I'm just exhausted. But I'm finally willing to ask for help, to seek accountability or support, and to acknowledge that I'm not broken or a disorganized person—I just need to ask for help and have a plan. I won't give up, even when I feel like I'm failing. I'm allowing God to teach me that something that doesn't come naturally to me is still good and I can do it.

At the beginning, I thought they would hate it, but I know kids and adults often have a bad attitude about new things before realizing it's not as bad as we thought it would be! I also thought I would forget to do it, but when I started doing it more and more, the kids would ask me to do it. And now that my kids are older, we read the Word of God and have conversations about it because we made the habit of reading. It has become something we connect over. Now my thirteen-year-old is studying the Bible, and he's encouraging me to study with him on a deeper level.

I know that God is making something beautiful just through my practice of reading to my kids, reading Scripture verses, reading the Bible, sharing how much I love the stories, and telling them how God has spoken into my life. Reading leads to moments where we stop to connect with the Bible and with each other.[2]

NATALIA TORRES

PART THREE

FAITH GROWTH CYCLE:

SPROUT STAGE

Sprout Stage

Seed Stage

Root Stage

ONCE I'VE CULTIVATED THE SOIL for my garden and ordered the right seeds, I'll want to plant those seeds. The packet of seeds is so full of potential, I might be tempted to just toss them into my freshly cultivated soil. But if I chuck seeds across the soil willy-nilly, I'll end up with plants sprouting in random places, an unmanageable jungle of confused growth instead of a tidy garden of intentional sprouts.

You might now have a clear vision for family discipleship, but a vision isn't enough. Writing out a lovely vision is like ordering a package of seeds in January: wonderful, but useless if there's no plan attached. If I don't plan where to put them in my garden and when to plant them, I'm never going to see growth. So while the vision is important, we can't stop here. Likewise, motivation and vision alone won't get your kids digging into the Bible. You might understand how to navigate the obstacles you're facing, but simply moving the impediment won't get you where you want to go.

That's why the Sprout Stage is so important. Now we're going to plan! And if that sounds daunting, don't worry—*this* plan doesn't involve long-term strategy or heavy investment. Instead, we're going to start by adding in *one thirty-second habit at a time*—because, as we'll discover, thirty-second habits are the solution to nearly all our obstacles. Our eventual goal is a collection of little habits that work together over time to create a culture of family discipleship.

But we still need a plan. While we may think that just flinging an initial thirty-second habit into the mix will result in the growth we're longing for, even moving into that first habit requires intentionality and a sustainable approach. Once you understand the process, you'll be able to stick with a few small, easy habits that make a big difference in your day.

Modern habit formation science shows us that the *best* way to implement any new habit is to start with the smallest possible version, and this method of leveraging small habits to move toward growth is helpful in all sorts of situations:

- If your spouse isn't a Christian or if they're not really interested in talking about faith at home, starting little won't step on any toes.
- If you're looking for a way to begin with teens, starting little creates natural openings in their lives to talk about faith.
- If your kids are tiny, starting little suits their short attention spans.

Starting little works for all kinds of families.

In the Sprout Stage, you want to create small, sustainable faith routines that help the seeds of the gospel grow. No more haphazardly trying fifteen new habits or devotional books and hoping something beautiful will grow out of it. Instead, our intentional little habits will create predictable, manageable ways for our family to flourish!

WHY START LITTLE?

Making Goals Easy

Growing up, I went to church at least three times per week: Sunday morning services (plural), Sunday evening, Wednesday night girls club, and, as I got older, Friday night youth group. But while I was raised in a Christian family and spent a lot of time in church, I don't recall many at-home conversations about God, faith, or the Bible. At school my closest friends were also Christians, but we didn't really talk about our faith either. When I got married and started having my own children, I came to an uncomfortable realization: I didn't know how to have natural conversations about God with them. From my many years in kids' ministry, I knew how to teach a kick-butt lesson in Sunday school, write prayer journals and curriculums, and lead someone else's child to Christ—but did I know how to talk about my faith in daily moments with my husband and kids? Nope.

Your story is likely different from mine, but unless you grew up in the kinds of circles where talking about faith is as natural as talking about the weather, you probably feel some of the same hesitation when it comes to faith conversations. I know an organic lifestyle of family discipleship is possible because I've watched friends for whom every moment of parenting is discipleship, every conversation an opportunity to help a child understand the gospel. And I have seen my own progress toward this goal: learning to inhale and exhale the goodness of God in everyday moments, through everyday habits, as God gently leads me step-by-step. I don't have it all figured out, but I have found a way forward that is full of grace, remains sustainable for my family, and consistently points us back to our good God.

Little faith habits are how we plant intentional seeds that will sprout in our kids' lives—and in our own lives. I've seen this happen again and again in my family.

Over the years, I felt God gently pointing out that the little things I was doing were slowly changing the trajectory of our family. A Christian school teacher remarked how much Bible knowledge our son has, the accumulation of a two-minute-per-day interactive Bible study we'd done since he was a preschooler.[1] Our kids began to bring up concepts from our thirty-second morning devotional long after breakfast was over. Our son's deep-seated school anxiety eased as God used the twenty-second verse I'd prayed over him. And even I found myself equipped for a conversation about the future with our teen, instinctively quoting Bible verses we had memorized together. Little habits have changed the way we live and breathe and speak.

Simple habits might seem shallow or insufficient, but their

consistency waters the seeds for fruitful family faith. As Sally Clarkson reminds us, "In the whole life of faith, one of the best ways to begin is simply to establish a rhythm of family habits that keep your home centered on God. The whole idea of these habits is that they are a regular heartbeat in the life of your home."[2]

Slowly but surely, these little habits will shape you into the kind of parent you want to be, creating a life where parenting feels like discipleship.

THE SCIENCE OF STARTING LITTLE

When our oldest was around six years old, I accidentally started a little habit. I wanted to start reading the Bible with our boys, and I decided we'd do it at the breakfast table because they were all occupied with eating. The accidental little habit was a devotional book with incredibly short devotions. Each devotion took me under thirty seconds to read. I was able to continue the habit even on days when dishes, dirty floors, and the racing clock shrunk my motivation to nearly nonexistent. And because our kids were less likely to grumble or tune out over thirty seconds than over a longer devotional, I wasn't deterred by feeling frustrated or demoralized.

In *Tiny Habits*, BJ Fogg shares that "over the last twenty years, I've found that the only consistent, sustainable way to grow big is to start small."[3] Why is that? It's because small is easy, sustainable, and deceptively powerful.

Dr. Fogg discovered that any human behavior has three aspects: motivation, ability, and prompt. You need to feel motivated to do the behavior, have the ability to do the behavior, *and* be prompted to begin the behavior.[4] If you have the ability and a prompt or reminder but no motivation, you won't do the behavior. If you are motivated and have the ability but aren't prompted to begin, the behavior won't happen. And if you're motivated and have something reminding you—but no idea what to do? Obviously, the behavior can't happen.[5]

While you need all three aspects for any behavior to happen, BJ Fogg discovered a useful connection: As behaviors become easier to do, you need less motivation to do them. You don't need to be highly motivated to pick up your phone and scroll Instagram because it's easy to do. A niggling feeling of boredom is enough motivation, so the mere sight of your phone prompts you to pick it up and swipe over to the app. Conversely, as a behavior becomes harder to do, you need a lot more motivation to do it. A niggling feeling of boredom would not inspire me to do one hundred push-ups. (If I'm honest, it wouldn't even inspire me to do one push-up.)

Let's apply this principle to discipleship behaviors. Which of these two options is easier: getting your child to do a Bible study workbook, or praying a Bible verse over your child? You may have the same amount of motivation and even the same prompt to do each behavior, but praying a Bible verse over your child requires less from you. And because it's easier, you need a lot less motivation to do it, which helps you keep going on days when your motivation is low. As Fogg notes,

> Keeping changes small and expectations low is how
> you design around fair-weather friends like motivation
> and willpower. When something is tiny, it's easy
> to do—which means you don't need to rely on the
> unreliable nature of motivation.[6]

You may eventually work up to Bible study workbooks with your child, but the most sustainable way to get there is to start with something small and easy.

HOW TO CREATE A LITTLE HABIT

What's a small, regular habit that has a surprisingly large impact on your life? Maybe you drink more water during the day when you fill a big bottle of water in the morning, or you find that breathing a prayer right after waking up helps your mental health, or you feel more rested if you turn on a worship playlist while driving the kids home from school.

One of my readers told me he turns on the dishwasher every night before bed. Another puts recipes on cards in a box right away instead of trying to find them online later. Yet another developed a habit of putting away her clothes right after taking them off. A friend of mine gives her toilet a quick swish with the brush every time she uses it, which means she never needs to worry about toilet stains when unexpected company comes over. (I should probably consider adopting that habit.) Little habits like these make a big difference in the cleanliness of their homes and their ability to find important things quickly.

What do all these little habits have in common? They are realistic, specific, and easy.

- **Realistic:** Make sure your little habit is something you care about and something that suits your family! Swishing toilets and making the bed are only realistic if you care about the results. If you don't care about consistently clean toilets and beds, these habits aren't realistic for you. Similarly, if you don't want to memorize Scripture right now, don't start there just because someone on social media made you feel like you should. Choose something else, like breath prayers at bedtime or worship music in the car. Pick something you care about.

- **Specific:** You can't just have a nebulous idea: Your little habit needs to be something you can picture in your mind. Instead of saying to herself *I'll clean the kitchen in the morning*, one of my readers gave herself a specific task she could easily imagine: emptying the dishwasher right after walking into the kitchen. Similarly, we can take a great vision like "read the Bible with my kids" and turn it into something specific like "open the Bible and read one verse after breakfast." We have more success with habits that are super specific.

- **Easy:** Motivation comes and goes, which means easy behaviors are more likely to become habits than hard ones. Our culture of productivity constantly screams "Go big or go home," and the overachievers among us cringe at the slow process of spiritual formation. But research shows that the best pathway to true life change is making little changes that add up over time. My friend didn't try to clean the whole bathroom each day—she focused on a simple swish of the toilet instead. This was so easy that she didn't have any excuse *not* to do it. Similarly, we want our initial faith habits to be so easy there's no reason *not* to do them.

So when we set out to create a little faith habit that fits our unique family, we need to run it through each of these lenses:

- Is it realistic? (Do I want to do this? Does it suit my family?)
- Is it specific? (Can I picture myself doing this?)
- Is it easy? (Can I do this even on a busy day?)

Do you have an idea in mind? Write the faith habit here:

_____

Now it's time to ensure we're making this habit as little and attainable as possible. Let's say that you wrote *I want to start reading the Bible as a family during supper.* If you immediately pull out the big Bible and read a chapter a day, you're probably going to lose steam quickly. Instead, how could you introduce the idea slowly, using the smallest possible habits?

Let's point a shrink ray at our desired habit. Can we zap it into an even smaller version of the habit?

I want to start reading the Bible as a family at supper.

zap

More specific: I will read a section from a children's Bible storybook at supper.

zap

More realistic: I will read a super short, highly engaging devotional every night at supper.

zap

Easier: I will read a single Bible verse each night after we pray for our food.

The key here is choosing something short—ideally something that takes less than a minute. If you need help, I've created a list of little faith behaviors you can try. (See appendix A: Ideas for Little Habits.)[7]

As you're thinking of the smallest possible version of a habit, you might start to wonder if it can possibly make a difference. But imagine that there's this heavy steel door sealing off possibilities for family faith conversations in your life. That door is labeled with all the struggles and obstacles: "Too busy," "Too ill-equipped," "No one cares," and "Nothing's worked before." Starting one little habit cracks the door open. That leverage shift means more little habits can push it open wider, until your obstacles fall away. You won't stay in this place of small habits forever, but you get to start little, pointing your little ones to the God who cares and is trustworthy, slowly building on their knowledge and understanding as they grow.

Once you understand how to boil your goals down to habits that are almost absurdly little, you'll be well on your way to creating ongoing fruitfulness in your family's faith life.

Jesus said,

"I am the vine; you are the branches. Those who remain in me, and I in them, will produce much fruit. For apart from me you can do nothing. . . . When you produce much fruit, you are my true disciples. This brings great glory to my Father."
JOHN 15:5, 8

As we intentionally abide in Jesus through the little habits we create, God will work in our kids' lives to grow good, lasting fruit.

· · · · · · · · · KEY POINTS · · · · · · · ·

- It's crucial to have a good system for making changes in your life.

- Simple habits might seem shallow or like they're not enough, but they will set the foundation for a family faith that is fruitful.

- As behaviors become easier to do, you need less motivation to do them.

- A new habit should be realistic, specific, and easy.

- You get to start little, pointing your little ones to the God who cares and is trustworthy, slowly building on their knowledge and understanding as they grow.

- Little habits have the power to crack into a busy routine and grow something big.

· · · · · · · · YOUR TURN · · · · · · · ·

1. What little habit already makes a big impact on your life?

_____

_____

2. What is the biggest struggle for you when it comes to faith habits: finding motivation, having the ability to do them, or remembering to do them?

_____

_____

3. What habit do you think God wants for your family right now?

_____

_____

4. What is one thing you want to remember from this chapter?

_____

_____

MAGGIE'S STORY

Our habit recipe was so simplistic, I thought that it would be easy to forget. Instead, it turned out to be so easy to remember! We would pray as soon as we got to our bus stop, and within a week our kids were reminding us if we forgot.

We ran into a hiccup when the weather warmed up and we would walk to the bus stop instead, but after two days of me quickly remembering as the bus pulled up, the kids were reminding us again.

We have seen their confidence grow in their own prayers since we started the habit. They are more willing to jump in with their own prayer requests and are excited when God answers them. It has been a great change in our lives![8]

MAGGIE ANDREWS

WHERE DO I START?

Finding a Keystone Habit

I'M SITTING ACROSS FROM A FRIEND at my kitchen table, sharing about a class for parents I taught over fourteen years ago at my church. She nods emphatically and says, "I know; I was there." I feel sheepish, but that feeling fades as she begins to tell me about her three daughters, all in their twenties now, and how they each changed profoundly because of what she learned from that class.

With a tear sliding down each cheek, she says, "My kids would not be who they are right now without it." She leans in. "When you ask God every single night to bless your kids . . . don't be surprised when he does."

And now we're both sniffling. A tiny little habit I discovered and taught before my own sons were even conceived is impacting these young women into their adult years, one of whom will soon be nurturing her own family.

This is far from an isolated story.

How is this possible? The habit my friend had used took only about twenty seconds a day. But that small, consistent practice equipped her and her family to move further and deeper into the faith formation she longed for.

There are times when the smallest, most sustainable habit begins to shift how your family interacts with God—those life-changing habits are called *keystone habits*. In architecture, a keystone is the piece in the middle of an arch, the piece that locks everything together and allows the arch to stand for decades to come. Or to put it another way, a keystone habit is like a pebble thrown into water: Ripples travel far beyond the initial impact, continuing to change lives long past the moment it begins.

Growing a flourishing faith doesn't just involve knowing how to create a habit; it means discerning which habits are most likely to last and to create space for ongoing growth. Once we understand the fundamentals of habit formation, we can take a deeper look at which ones have the potential for the most impact.

THE POWER OF KEYSTONE HABITS

Several years ago, as my husband and I drove to a weekend getaway in the mountains, we listened to an audiobook I had downloaded from the library: *The Power of Habit* by Charles Duhigg. The more I heard, the more excited I got. My husband snickered as I literally bounced in the passenger seat, thrilled by the connections I was making between habit formation and family faith.

The biggest aha moment? This book introduced me to keystone habits: very simple habits that have the power to unlock huge changes in your life.

Duhigg shared about a study where the researchers simply asked people prone to overeating to write down what they ate, one day per week. *That's so absurdly simple*, you might be thinking. *How could that really make a difference?* But over time, some of the participants began to record their food intake more than once a week. Then they began to create meal plans. Then they started writing healthy grocery lists.

With every new habit, these people who had long struggled with their relationship with food began to lose weight. The researchers hadn't asked them to do anything but that first simple habit: writing down their food intake one day per week. But with this simple win, participants realized that they were capable of bigger changes. Success with one small habit created a structure for other habits to flourish—which helped participants develop a pattern of healthier living.

A keystone habit tends to be one we might immediately discount because of its seeming insignificance. It seems too small to make a difference—and yet the ripple effect can be immense. As Duhigg wrote,

> Keystone habits say that success doesn't depend on getting every single thing right, but instead relies on identifying a few key priorities and fashioning them into powerful levers. . . . The habits that matter most are the ones that, when they start to shift, dislodge and remake other patterns.[1]

To explore how keystone habits work, we're going to look at an actual habit I've seen have significant impact in families: praying a biblical blessing over your child at bedtime. When I first saw that this practice had power, I could not figure out why—until I discovered the concept of a keystone habit. Like any good keystone habit, blessing your child is quick, easy to do, and easy to remember—and has a surprising power to, in Duhigg's words, "shift, dislodge and remake other patterns."

HOW KEYSTONE HABITS WORK

Everything on the planet obeys Newton's first law of motion, which says that an object at rest stays at rest and an object in motion stays in motion at the same trajectory. This is called *inertia*. The only way to overcome inertia is for another force to act on the object. (Imagine a baseball being thrown in space. It will keep going on its path until something knocks it off course.) Similarly, humans tend to resist change. We want to keep doing what we're doing, and it takes another force to change our behaviors. But just like small particles of space dust would be enough to change the course of our baseball, small habits have the power to change the course of a whole family. There are three reasons keystone habits can be the small force that changes the course of your family life: small wins, structures for other habits, and a new family culture.[2] Let's look at each in turn, and at how a bedtime blessing habit demonstrates each one.

Reason #1: Small Wins

Keystone habits offer small wins that help us realize bigger changes are possible.

When you find a keystone habit that works for your family, you keep doing it even when you're busy because it's easy. Praying a biblical blessing over your child can be as simple as taping a Bible verse to the wall above your child's bed, then reading that verse out loud to your child when you're tucking them in. Anyone can do it. Suddenly, you're experiencing a small win, and you start to get excited about what you can do next.

A friend started praying the same Bible verse over each of her four kids every night, and over time, she noticed that they were sleeping better and waking up happier. Because their mornings were better, she was able to start reading the Bible with them before school, which eventually grew into a twenty-minute time of teaching and conversation. The small win created a positive ripple effect and gave her hope that bigger changes were in reach.

Reason #2: Structures for Other Habits

Keystone habits create structures where other habits can flourish. If your family's spiritual life is like that steel door closed firmly shut, a keystone habit such as the nightly biblical blessing cracks the door open. And once you open the door—even just a tiny bit—swinging it open further and stepping through becomes far easier.

A simple habit creates a place in your day that allows other habits—like a nightly devotion or Bible discussion time—to take root. A few years ago, a reader emailed to tell me her biggest struggle was finding time to disciple her kids. She wanted to start doing devotions with her kids but always got sidetracked and couldn't stay consistent. They had even purchased a new family devotional at Christmas . . . and only got through four lessons over two months. A few months later, she posted in my Facebook group that she had decided to start praying biblical blessings over her kids. She and her husband picked seven verses, one for each night of the week. The kids loved it and reminded them if they forgot. Eventually, the family decided to add in that new devotional again, just once per week. Because they already had the blessings habit, this new habit felt like a natural fit. Within a few months, they were reading a devotion every night. When the family finished the first devotional, they purchased a second one to go through together. Their entire family now looks forward to this time. The keystone habit created a structure and then momentum: Once it was part of the family rhythm, other faith-forming activities easily followed.

Reason #3: A New Family Culture

Praying a Bible verse over your children at bedtime might not look like much on the outside, but the practice of consistently pointing your kids to God creates a new culture in your family. Your children learn that the Bible is important, that God is important, and that both have a direct effect on their lives.

With the blessing keystone habit, parent after parent tells me how their kids consistently remind them to pray the blessing at bedtime. One little one asks for a second blessing if she gets out of bed for any reason. A teen asked his parents to speak it over him just before life-changing surgery. Even my friends with older teenagers say their kids will remind them if they forget the blessing at bedtime. Why? *Because the keystone habit has created a culture of faith.*

And once you've established a family culture, the priorities of that culture spill over into other aspects of your life. A biblical blessing helps turn the Bible from a book on the shelf into something living and active, which then normalizes going to the Bible at other times in your day. When hard conversations come your way, the language of the blessing has already formed a neural pathway of speaking goodness and building trust, allowing deeper faith conversations to happen more naturally.

FIND YOUR KEYSTONE

A small keystone habit—like twenty seconds spent praying a biblical blessing over your child every night—has an unexpectedly large impact. However, a nightly blessing is not the only habit that can become a keystone in your family.

Are your kids consistently sullen on the ride home from school? You might turn on a movie or allow them tech time just to survive the drive with their grumpy, overstimulated selves. But what might happen if you turned on worship music? It's a very small win that only requires you to push a button. Your kids might still opt to stare at a device, but if you take those moments to worship instead of worry or nag about homework, your own heart will change. Seeing you worship day after day, even just for five minutes, will change their own attitudes. The lyrics will seep into their own hearts, and they'll come to expect a more worshipful, gentler parent. This changes the culture of your drive home and could lead to other habits, like conversation or prayer.

Perhaps your kids are too young for school, but you have been trying to read the Bible with your toddlers in the afternoon. They squirm and beg for snacks, and it's a miserable experience. But what might happen if you fed them a snack *during* your Bible-reading time? It's a small tweak that gives you a win. Snacktime discipleship shifts a culture of combative discipleship into one of joy and gives you a place in your day to add new faith habits, like Bible memory, worship, and prayer.

One last example. Do your kids struggle with bedtime? They ask for three more glasses of water and seventeen more books, then cling like burrs when you try to leave. What might happen if you play the grateful game each night? In the grateful game, you take turns shouting (or whispering) something you want to thank God for. The grateful game is a simple, fun way to help kids move past bedtime anxiety. In *Raising Prayerful Kids*, one of the authors shares how playing this game in the car led to a family culture of gratitude.[3] It could also easily lead to other types of prayer, making it yet another powerful keystone habit.

What keystone habit do you want to try? You may want to look back at the habit you thought about in the last chapter to see if you think it will work as a keystone, or you can pop back to appendix A for more ideas. If you like the idea of blessing your children at night, appendix B: The Blessing Habit (beginning on page 165) lays out more about the how and why.

Once you've landed on a keystone habit that is realistic, specific, and easy, write it down here because we're going to create a supporting framework for it in the upcoming chapter.

My keystone habit: _____

Next, you're going to troubleshoot your keystone habit. To do that, ask yourself two questions:

1. What will make this habit difficult?
2. How can I make this habit easier?

Answering these questions will help you make your keystone habit as easy as possible. Let's start with our keystone habit example: praying a Bible verse over your child at bedtime:

1. What will make this habit difficult? *Flipping through my Bible to find the verse as we're trying to do the rest of our bedtime routine.*

2. How can I make this habit easier? *I'll find a verse ahead of time, write it on a sticky note, and stick it above my child's bed.*

Now it's your turn. Imagine you want to read the Bible with your children after breakfast. Use these questions to identify what might hinder you and what would solve that issue:

1. What will make this habit difficult?

   _____

2. How can I make this habit easier?

   _____

When I was answering this question, I realized that digging for my Bible would eat up a lot of time and probably make me not want to follow through on reading with my kids. To make the habit easier, I put my Bible in the middle of my table and left it there. That became its place. I also put a bookmark in it so I could find my spot easily.

Okay, now that you've had some practice, apply these questions to your own keystone habit!

1. What will make this habit difficult?

   _____

2. How can I make this habit easier?

   _____

Sometimes the thing that makes a habit difficult is our own limiting beliefs. You might be thinking, *I can't do this because my spouse isn't on board.* Or *It feels awkward to do this with my family.* If the thing that's holding you back is your own thought patterns, make sure to pop back to chapters 3 and 5 to remind yourself of what's true.

If you try the habit and find it's not working the way you hoped, then it's probably not your keystone! Finding a keystone habit that works for your unique family is a journey, not something you have to get perfect on the first try. Think of this process as a science experiment you're carrying out on your family. A scientist always makes a hypothesis about what will happen, but if it doesn't turn out quite right, they don't throw a tantrum and walk away. They re-examine their assumptions and tweak the hypothesis, then try the experiment again. You can do the same! If it doesn't turn out the way you expect, you have permission to reassess and tweak until you find something that works.

Keystone habits are small, sustainable habits that shift how our family interacts with God because they disrupt our patterns and create a chain reaction of changes. They also remind us that "success doesn't depend on getting every single thing right,"[4] which is a blessing to busy parents because it releases us from the pressure to do family discipleship in a specific way. And this is the good news: Implementing one keystone habit *that suits our family's needs* will result in changes far more quickly and effectively than trying to become a perfect parent could ever do.

• • • • • • • • • KEY POINTS • • • • • • • •

A keystone family faith habit

- gives you a small, easy win that shows that bigger change is possible;
- creates a structure for other habits to flourish; and
- creates a culture of faith in your home.

• • • • • • • • • YOUR TURN • • • • • • • •

1. What time of day does your family tend to struggle?

   _____

   _____

2. Is there a keystone habit that could change this difficult time into a small win?

   _____

   _____

3. Ask God, "How could you use this habit to change that time of day for our whole family?" Record what comes to mind.

   _____

   _____

4. What is one thing you want to remember from this chapter?

   _____

   _____

HEATHER'S STORY

When I first started praying a blessing over my kids, I was worried. Would it feel weird and awkward? What if my kids didn't want me doing it? I also worried that I would forget or do it for a short time and then let the habit go as life got busier. There are always so many things to do.

What actually happened? Our children love it! They didn't quite know what to think the first night, but they welcomed it the second night. One thing I've noticed is that there are fewer power struggles at bedtime now. Kids willingly get in bed with smiles on their faces. They rush to be first and will even physically place our hand upon their heads. And they all seem to be sleeping well! We have done it almost every night for over three months now. The kids love it and have the shorter blessings memorized (even our three-year-old has the fruit of the Spirit memorized!). They even ask to bless us in return.

My husband has taken more ownership of this habit now as well. On nights when I'm busy cleaning the kitchen and we need to get the kids to bed, my husband does the blessings. Other nights, we take turns or do it together. My husband has said multiple times how much he loves that we're blessing our children. I feel that it's bringing us all closer together.[5]

HEATHER JOLLY

HOW DO I KEEP GOING?

Determining Prompts and Rewards

SEVERAL YEARS AGO, when I wanted to start reading the Bible at breakfast time with my kids, I knew *what* I wanted but not *how* to make it happen. My mornings were hectic with a capital *H*! I would wake up after my children, then I would dash around grabbing food and changing diapers and helping kids get dressed and emptying the dishwasher, then rush to drop everyone off at the right places.

I disliked who I was in the mornings. I was irritable and impatient. I desperately wanted to start reading the Bible with my kids in the mornings, but *I. Just. Couldn't.* Even when I had the time, I would empty the dishwasher instead of sitting down at the table.

And I knew that even if I managed to read the Bible once or twice, it would be all too easy for other tasks to push out the one I was trying to fit in. Motivation had only taken me so far in the past because something else would come along that would be momentarily more motivating and I'd veer off course.

Our eventual practice of short devotions wouldn't have turned into a little habit if I hadn't figured out two problems. The first—keeping us from even getting off the ground—was that I had no consistent pattern. Any new, good habits had no chance to take hold thanks to my current bad habits of late waking, disorganization, and distractedness. I had an admirable goal, but how could I remember how to do it? The second problem was that I needed to make sure I had enough motivation to keep going. Once I started my habit, how could I ensure I wouldn't get derailed like I had so often before?

THE POWER OF PROMPTS

We get out of bed because we need to turn off the alarm or use the toilet. We eat because we're hungry or bored. We get in the car to go to work or school because we look at the time and are reminded to get going.

If you look carefully at your life, you'll notice that every behavior has an invisible prompt. Habit research tells us the reason for that: We all need *something* to trigger a behavior. This *something* is called a *prompt*. To grow those deep faith roots in your family, you'll want to harness the power of prompts.

Remember, every behavior needs the same three components: motivation, ability, and a prompt.[1] Determining your prompt is critical when you're planning out a new habit because without a prompt, your new behavior is dead in the water. It'll never become a habit because you'll rarely remember to do it!

So what *are* prompts (also known as cues or triggers), anyway? There are three types of prompts:[2]

1. **External Prompts.** An external prompt is something we see or hear that reminds us to do a behavior: for example, an alarm clock or a school bell, a child's cry or a calendar reminder on your phone. External prompts don't usually work well for habits because they're far too easy to ignore. I mean, how many times have you hit the snooze button in the morning or forgotten a dentist appointment because you missed (or ignored) your external prompt?

   Several years ago I would have attributed the success of my Bible and Breakfast habit to an external prompt: a huge plate my husband and I happened upon at one of those "paint your own pottery" shops in a mall. I painted the plate with little stalks of wheat up the sides to remind me of the Bread of Life, and then I used the plate as a consistent spot for my Bible in the center of the table. However, I've since realized that the plate was only part of the equation. Yes, seeing it reminded me of my priority, but it wasn't enough to establish my habit—because, as an external prompt, it was too easy to ignore.

2. **Internal Prompts.** The second type of prompt is internal, like a feeling of hunger. Internal prompts can also be thoughts like *I should call my mother* or *I haven't had much water today—I should have some before I feel dehydrated.* Most internal prompts are also easy to ignore. How many times have you shushed that little voice that noticed your neck muscles were tight and suggested you might feel better if you took a stretch break? Every day I used to think, *I should sit down and read with my kids*, but that internal prompt was easy to set aside when I looked around and saw all the other things I needed to do.

3. **Anchor Prompts.** The best kind of prompts for long-lasting behavior change are what BJ Fogg calls *anchors*.[3] An anchor is something that you already do all the time—an existing habit. And before you say, "I don't have any existing habits," let me ask you this: Did you . . .

get up this morning?

use the bathroom today?

brush your teeth?

eat today?

go to bed last night?

shower today?

If you did any of those things, you have existing habits that anchor your day.

When it comes to identifying anchor prompts that can help in family discipleship, you can ask yourself this question: *What routines, tasks, and rhythms already exist with my kids?* Whether you're homeschooling, dropping kids off before work and picking them up after, or serving as a permanent taxi driver for active teens, you're already doing many consistent, ordinary tasks with your kids daily.

So how can we use the power of anchors to invite God into what we're already doing?

How to Use Velcro Prompts

If you've ever potty trained a child, you've worked to instill a critical habit because you know it's a key part of being healthy: washing hands after using the toilet. (Aren't you glad your parents instilled that habit in you?)

But for this habit to stick, you don't just tell your child to wash their hands. They'd probably forget, or they'd remember at odd times, like three o'clock in the morning. Rather, after they use that little plastic potty, you stand in the bathroom with them, lathering their chubby little hands and helping them scrub and rinse. You know that for handwashing to be a healthy habit, they have to experience doing it *after* using the potty, over and over, until it simply becomes part of the overall routine. You eventually incorporate a third simple habit into that routine: flushing the toilet. Again, you don't want them to randomly flush the toilet during the day or flush it when they first walk into the bathroom. Rather, you teach your little ones to use the toilet, *then* flush, *then* wash. If you've done that, and your child flushes and washes their hands even when you're not around, you already know how effective it is to connect old and new habits together.

Habit formation expert James Clear calls this *habit stacking*, because you "identify a current habit you already do each day and then stack your new behavior on top."[4] I like to imagine sticking one piece of velcro to a piece that's already on the wall: attaching the new habit to the anchor habit.

Let's say you wanted to say a quick prayer each morning. The worst way to remember to do this is to rely on an internal prompt—in other words, thinking, *Oh, I'll just remember.* Simply *trying* to remember something rarely works. The second worst way to remind yourself would be to set an alarm for six o'clock every morning. I don't know about you, but it would take about one day before I'd start hitting snooze on that alarm. Those external prompts are too easily ignored.

The best way to remember is to fasten your desired habit to a habit you already have. Your anchor habit could be "the moment I swing my feet onto the floor," no matter what the actual time is. Then you fasten the prayer habit to the anchor so it sticks. The old habit and the new habit connect like this: *As soon as my feet touch the floor, I will say a quick prayer.*

Personally, that anchor doesn't work for me because I don't even know what day it is when I wake up. But perhaps the anchor could be stepping into the shower, putting on your slippers, or applying your makeup. Whatever simple rhythm you already do every day can be your first piece of velcro. The second is your new, desired behavior.

I didn't understand the power of anchors back when I was trying to establish my Bible and Breakfast habit, but I inadvertently ended up developing one: "after I sit down to eat." When I sat down to eat breakfast, I would immediately open our short devotional and read it between bites. Now I can't sit down to eat breakfast with my kids without feeling the need to read the Bible with them! My two pieces of velcro are stuck tight.

How to Find an Anchor

Once you understand anchoring prompts, you'll discover how easy it is to slip new, positive behaviors into your day. You won't have to worry about remembering to read the Bible with your kids because your anchor will prompt you.

What's an anchor in your day? Think back to the keystone habit you chose in the last chapter. You will do this behavior *after* a specific prompt that reliably occurs in your day. Attaching your new habit to your prompt sounds like this: "*After* I [experience prompt], I will [do little habit]."

Effective anchors are more specific than you might expect. James Clear advises that "the more tightly bound your new habit is to a specific cue, the better the odds are that you will notice when the time comes to act."[5] For example, you may have thought "as I put my kids to bed" would be a good anchor for when you want to read a Bible storybook with your kids, but it's actually a little nebulous. Will you read the Bible storybook while you're changing their clothes? While they're lying in bed? While you're chasing them around the room? What exactly counts as "putting my kids to bed," anyway? Instead, you'll want to choose a prompt that is so specific you can see the moment in your mind. You might choose to read a Bible storybook with your kids as soon as they finish pulling their pj's on. The sight of them in their cute pj's now becomes your cue to open the book. (Of course, this doesn't work if your kids tend to choose not to change into pajamas, which I may or may not know about from personal experience.)

For a noncomprehensive list of suggestions for good anchors, check out appendix C: Ideas for Prompts and Rewards. As you consider the list or other anchors you notice about your day, ask God, "How can I invite you into what I'm already doing?" Then fill in the blanks:

After I _____,

I will _____.

Once you begin noticing anchors in your life, you'll realize you're a lot more consistent than you thought! There are so many things we do each day without even thinking about them, and those are the habits that make excellent anchors for our new habits.

THE POWER OF REWARDS

My boys enjoy watching Mark Rober's engineering experiment videos on YouTube, where he uses his NASA engineering skills to tackle wild projects like converting a leaf blower into a snow-ball machine gun or building a dartboard that senses the dart and moves so the player can get a bull's-eye on every try. I love how this sense of fun informs how Rober thinks about finding solutions to problems he encounters. He calls it the Super Mario Effect. Essentially, instead of focusing on the frustration of the setbacks (like the cliffs and obstacles in the Super Mario games), he focuses on the goal (like saving Princess Peach). Instead of looking at the problems and being frustrated by the failures, he moves forward, treating each new problem like a game to be solved.[6]

I think we need some of this perspective in our faith-formation practices. The stakes of the game are so high! But while we have a part to play, God is the one guiding the story forward, which means we all need to take a deep breath. Only God can ultimately draw our kids' hearts toward himself, which means the pressure is off us to "get it right." We're important . . . but not mission critical. Having a little fun with the process isn't just allowed—it's a key part of the game.

Playfulness is important when we're discipling young children because it helps keep them engaged. But what if I told you that *enjoyment* is a critical part of habit formation?

Think back to when you first started using your favorite social media or messaging platform. It was fun, right? You enjoyed connecting with old friends and posting pictures of your cat. You found memes and videos that made you laugh so hard you just had to share them with a friend. Yes, social media certainly comes with its problems, but it can also be truly fun.

Now think back to how long it took social media to become a habit in your life. Did it take twenty-one days? Forty days?

Probably more like forty minutes, right? The moment you got the first thumbs-up or heart, you were hooked.

Social media becomes a habit so easily because of how habits become wired into our brains. Each habit researcher talks about habits slightly differently, but it boils down to the basic habit loop: there's a cue (or prompt), then a routine (or behavior), then a reward.[7] Without a reward, the behavior simply won't become a habit. If we didn't immediately get those hearts on Instagram, checking the app probably wouldn't become a habit quite as easily. That's why *joy* is so vital to family discipleship: faith activities need to be rewarded if they're going to become habits, and joy is an excellent reward.

But if we're honest, often our spiritual habits have very little immediate payoff. (There's a reason they're usually called spiritual *disciplines*.) Similar to pursuing a discipline like learning the piano, the rewards occur in the long run, not immediately, even if you practice daily.

So if we and our kids don't see the rewards of our faith formation for a long time—if all we have is the prompt and the behavior—how can we complete the habit loop? If our kids are grumpy or uninterested, if saying the Lord's Prayer for the twentieth time doesn't spark any joy, or if you'd rather just toss the kids into bed without trying to get them to settle down for a devotional, how does all this become a true habit?

How Celebrations Become Rewards

Several years ago, we adopted the sweetest dog from a local rescue. With her big, floppy ears and loving personality, she had our hearts immediately. We adored her . . . at least, until we took her for walks. She practically tore our arms off anytime we walked her in our neighborhood, dragging me to my knees on multiple occasions when she spotted a fellow canine or a rabbit. We finally hired a trainer, who trained our family as we attempted to train the dog. That's when we learned about the power of a consistent, immediate reward.

Let's imagine that I said to my pup, "You ignore that dog, and I'll give you a big treat when you get home!" Do you think she would have listened? Nope! She needed the third part of the habit loop: an immediate reward.

Her old habit loop looked like this:

- *Cue*: dog on the street
- *Behavior*: lunge and bark
- *Reward*: the dog says hello by lunging and barking back

To change her habit, I needed to rewire her brain with a new habit loop:

- *Cue*: dog on the street
- *Behavior*: walk nicely beside Mom
- *Reward*: delicious treat

We learned to treat her every time she did what we wanted, and though it's taken time, she's now at the point where she sees a dog on the sidewalk and looks at me for a treat, drool already dripping off her tongue.

We may be more advanced than dogs, but the habit routine works the same way in our brains. You and your kids need immediate rewards too. BJ Fogg calls this *celebration*:

When you celebrate effectively, you tap into the reward circuitry of your brain. By feeling good at the right moment, you cause your brain to recognize and encode the sequence of behaviors you just performed. In other words, you can hack your brain to create a habit by celebrating and self-reinforcing.[8]

Our brains seek out behaviors that make us feel good—God *created* us that way! Celebration acknowledges that God created our brains to want to do things that make us feel good. We can partner with God to create cue-routine-reward systems that change the trajectory of our family life. Rewards for family faith might look like the inherent joy our kids get from marching around the kitchen island and tooting imaginary horns, trying to bring it down like the walls of Jericho. The reward might be as simple as brewing hot chocolate for any child who wants to read the Bible alongside us or passing out new funky pens and colorful highlighters for an activity. A reward can even be intangible, like noticing a sense of peace after praying together. When we intentionally celebrate our faith habits, we're using the way God made our brains for good.

How to Create Instant Celebrations

What if saying the Lord's Prayer with your kids doesn't naturally give you a spiritual high? Even if a family faith habit doesn't bring inherent joy and there's no way to make it playful, you can easily make yourself feel good about a behavior: Just create an instant celebration for yourself!

Here's how it works. Let's say you want to say the Lord's Prayer with your child at bedtime. You choose as your anchor something like "after I sit down on her bed to say good night," and then you say the Lord's Prayer.

Next, before you do anything else, reach over and give your child a hug or a high five. That will bring a smile to both of you and release the hormones that make you feel good. And just like that, you've created a powerful connection binding that prompt, behavior, and celebration. The next time you kneel to say good night, your brain and her brain will both say, "Hey, let's do that thing that made me feel good!" You might still need to remind yourself the first few times, but it'll get wired in extra fast when you practice celebration.

It may not be realistic to give your child a hug after every behavior you want to turn into a habit (especially if your child doesn't like hugs). You'll discover what celebrations work best for your unique family. And you can also celebrate on your own! Feel free to celebrate the moment you *remember* to do the behavior. When you find ways to celebrate, you'll get an immediate sense of accomplishment and satisfaction that your mind will remember the next time you're fighting through a tough moment with your child. (For a list of suggestions, check out appendix C: Ideas for Prompts and Rewards.) Once you get started, you'll discover countless ways to celebrate.

Write down a celebration your child will love, as well as one that makes you feel good:

How I will celebrate with my child: _____

How I will celebrate on my own: _____

PUTTING IT ALL TOGETHER

Over the course of the Sprout Stage, you've discovered the power of little faith habits in your life. You learned how to pick a habit that is realistic and sustainable and how to determine whether a habit can be a keystone. You discovered how to pair a habit with an anchor that occurs naturally in your day and how instant celebrations make habits stick even faster. Now it's time to put it all together to form your habit plan.

First, look back at each stage of your habit brainstorming over the last three chapters and record your ideas here. If you've refined or changed something along the way, that's fine! This space should reflect the journey you've been on so far.

My Habit Ideas

My keystone habit: _____

What will make this habit difficult? _____.

How can I make this habit easier? _____

My revised keystone habit: _____

My anchor: _____

How I will celebrate with my child: _____

How I will celebrate on my own: _____

We can now put together our whole habit plan!

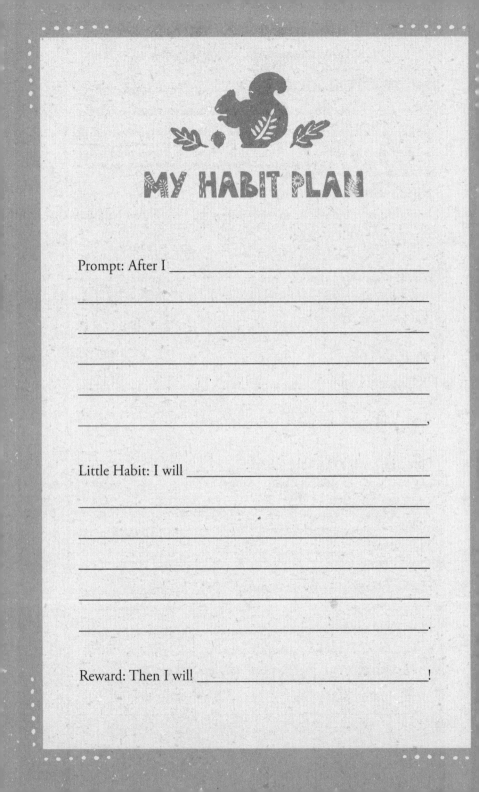

MY HABIT PLAN

Prompt: After I _____

_____

_____

_____

_____

_____,

Little Habit: I will _____

_____

_____

_____

_____

_____.

Reward: Then I will! _____!

KEY POINTS

- Every behavior in our lives has a prompt.

- The best way to remember to do your new behavior is to connect it to a habit you already have.

- Another way to think about prompts: How can I invite God into what I'm already doing?

- Choose a prompt that is so specific you can see it in your mind.

- Without a reward, the behavior simply won't become a habit.

- You can create instant celebrations for habits that don't naturally feel rewarding.

YOUR TURN

1. What anchor do you already use for personal spiritual formation? (For example, you might pour a cup of coffee and then sit down with your Bible; put your seat belt on and turn on a sermon podcast; or hit an icy patch while driving and pray for safety.)

2. Is there a time in your day that you'd love to invite God into, but it seems impossible to change?

3. What kind of instant celebration makes the most sense for your personality?

_____

_____

4. What is one thing you want to remember from this chapter?

_____

_____

LEAH'S STORY

I decided I wanted to practice a memory verse with my boys when we got to the bus stop, as we usually have to wait a few minutes for the bus. It felt good to send them off with a blessing for their day. To celebrate our habit, I'd let them each give me their hardest high five after practicing. That one idea has helped tremendously in making our new habit not feel like a chore or burden. The boys love to give me the hardest high fives! Even as we've learned more verses, the high-five joy has not worn off—it continues to give them the motivation to memorize a new verse each time![9]

LEAH MARTIN

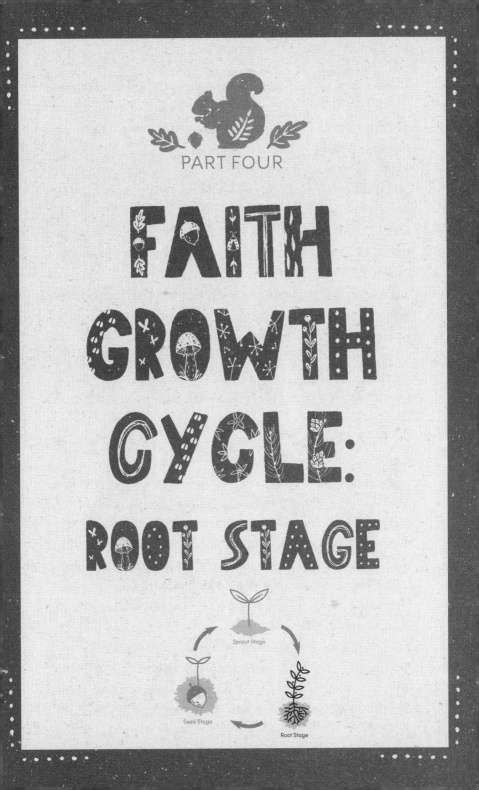

EVERY PLANT IN MY GARDEN has specific needs. If I want to care well for each plant, I should pick up a book on gardening so I can discover the specific needs of a tomato plant or a rosebush and act accordingly.

By the time we reach the Root Stage, we've planted seeds and watched them sprout, and now we need to learn how to deepen our little habits through caring for the different needs and learning styles in our home. Doing intentional work to root our habits ensures they become life-giving rhythms of faith instead of empty, legalistic rituals.

Don't feel pressured to rush through this stage or do more before your child is ready! We have eighteen years with these kids, and just like tree roots, faith roots take a long time to grow. You don't need to stress about teaching your preschooler systematic theology (although if that's where God leads you, go for it). You get to start little and point your little one to the God who cares for them and is trustworthy. Parenting isn't a race to the finish line—it's a long, slow hike with detours and good conversations and lots of snacks.

In *Habits of the Household*, Justin Whitmel Earley reminds us that "caring about how habits are shaping your family is not legalistic. What would be legalistic is saying that God loves you more because of your habits. Or that you can earn your salvation by picking the right habits."[1] It's the approach that makes the difference between spiritual disciplines and legalistic rituals. However, once we get those new habits in our lives, sometimes we can feel like we're in a rut. Our faith habits can become empty, legalistic rituals instead of life-giving rhythms of faith.

Therefore, in the Root Stage, we learn how to take those little habits we formed in the Sprout Stage and make them deeper and richer. There are many ways to expand on your little habits, so again, you'll want to make sure you're following God's lead to help you find the right spiritual root boosters for your family instead of trying to do everything. One of those root boosters is nudging our kids toward spiritual independence, but there are other ways to deepen their faith as well. As your kids engage consistently and with creativity, their roots will grow deeper into Christ.

HOW DO I GO DEEPER?

Keeping Habits Vibrant

WHEN I TAUGHT PIANO for several years after finishing university, I discovered a few things about learning an instrument that I hadn't really noticed as a child. We all know that to learn to play piano well, you need to sit down every day and practice a bit. But as part of that, you need to master several fundamental habits that might feel overly basic or simple. You'll learn to read a new visual language of musical notes and translate that to the keyboard. (Even if you're learning to play by ear, you'll still need to practice enough to understand chords and key signatures and where the notes are on the piano.) You'll practice fingering patterns and scales until your brain knows what note you're on even when your hands are covered. Only once you have the basics down can you start adding dynamics, introducing more complex pieces, or writing your own music.

Your first little faith habits are the basics, and eventually they will become automatic. Your hands will lift to pray over your kids as they tie their shoelaces. You will buckle everyone into the van and immediately start singing your memory verse. You will tuck your child in and automatically lean over to bless them. And you will rejoice because you'll see your family changing as these little moments accumulate.

God made our brains to love habits because these automatic responses free them to deal with other problems. But imagine if a committed pianist continued to play only basic scales over and over for years. They'd be bored out of their mind, right? Similarly, when a family faith habit becomes automatic, you may begin noticing that a practice that used to delight your children now makes their eyes glaze over.

If you've settled into some great faith habits as a family but you're starting to feel like they're becoming a little stagnant, like you're chafing at the routine, or like your kids just need a little bit more, it's time to get rooted. The Root Stage involves a lot less of "follow these steps" and lot more of "listen to God" because, as my friend Gretchen says,

> God stubbornly doesn't give us instructions that would send us in any direction except total and complete dependence on him.
> We are meant to live a Spirit-led life, not a formula-driven life.[1]

If we want our children to develop a lifelong faith to call their own, we can't stay in the Sprout Stage. Once our habits have become automatic, we still have to be intentional about them. The Root Stage helps us be purposeful in a new way and keep our family faith formation moving forward.

THREE WAYS TO BECOME ROOTED

Have you ever picked up your Bible and realized you were reading it merely out of habit and not getting anything out of it? Congratulations: You've discovered the dark side of a habit.

The bright side of your Bible-reading habit is that you're doing it. But when it has become just another "thing" to do—that's the dark side. If you pray the same blessing over your child night after night for years, the words may become so familiar to you both that they lose all meaning. Any of our faith habits can become rote, even legalistic.

Creating those first habits doesn't mean we can now disciple our kids on autopilot. Now that we don't need to spend all our energy on simply *remembering* to do a habit, we get to go deeper. When it's time to root a habit, we can ask God to help us expand our Bible reading, choose a different verse to pray over our kids, or invite our kids into more intentional worship.

So how do we root a habit?

I'm not a betting person, but if I were, I would bet that I could walk into any store with Christian parenting books and 99.9 percent of them would be about this stage of faith development. In recent years, two such books helped me bring my kids deeper into prayer, another challenged me to research the historic Christian calendar, another helped me talk about racism with my kids in a gospel-focused way, and some helped me think through apologetics with my kids. If you're looking for a way to root your child's faith in a specific area, you'll discover no shortage of books, resources, and podcasts that will help. (Check out appendix D: Rooted Resources for some topical resources I've found helpful!)

To deepen those little habits you've already started, though, we'll explore a framework of three different ways you can build on any family faith habit.

1. Make it longer.

One way to deepen small faith habits is to extend the length of time in the habit. Perhaps we've successfully started a one-minute Bible and Breakfast habit, but now we'd like to help our kids take it deeper. The bit-by-bit approach hasn't changed—we're not talking about suddenly jumping to marathon-length Bible reading here. Even after we start, we'll continue to grow in small increments. So what does incremental growth look like?

- Instead of reading one Bible verse at breakfast, you now read two or three.

- If you're used to short, memorized prayers, switch to a slightly longer memorized prayer.

- If you've been memorizing very short Scriptures, choose a longer passage.

- Read the same passage twice, in the style of *lectio divina.*

We want to find that sweet spot where kids feel challenged but not overwhelmed. They probably won't even notice we've lengthened the reading or prayer time a smidge. But when we slowly make our habit longer, over time we'll see a difference in their spiritual growth.

2. Make it more complex.

Another way to deepen faith habits is to introduce more complexity to the existing habit. Here are some examples:

- When you read a Bible passage together, research the historical context or explore different interpretations with your child.

- Ask your child to look up the passage in their own Bible, helping them learn how to find the book, chapter, and verse.

- Introduce a new prayer style, such as the ACTS prayer pattern, that requires more focus and engagement.[2]

- Invite your kids to create their own worship music.

- Throw in some fun games or activities or even (gasp) Bible study workbooks that help them learn more about their faith.

- Teach your child how to turn a Scripture verse into a prayer (this is especially appropriate with the Psalms).

- Invite your child to create Bible verse artwork while listening to you read a devotional or Scripture passage.

Finding more complex approaches to a simple habit can help your child develop a richer understanding of their faith and strengthen their spiritual growth.

3. Attach another habit.

Attaching new habits to our existing ones is how we grew our original habits in the first place! We can use the same principle to add a new habit that complements the existing one.

- If your family reads a Bible passage together each night, you might add an opening prayer or end with a prayer of gratitude or a moment of silent reflection.

- If you read a Bible passage together, or if your child already reads the Bible regularly on their own, you could introduce Bible journaling, where your child writes down their thoughts and prayers about what they've read.

- If your child loves to listen to worship music, help them learn the lyrics so they can sing along.

- If you normally pray at the kitchen table, you could light a candle beforehand to remind you that Jesus, the Light of the World, is with you.

- If you pray a blessing over your child at bedtime, you could read a short devotional just before the final blessing.

Linking different kinds of faith habits together will help your kids connect the different aspects of their faith and strengthen their faith journey.

Starting one little habit can lead to a strong foundation of faith for your kids. God takes our little steps and extends them, through his mighty power, into an incredible journey over time. As my kids grow, I know their faith lives will look a bit different from mine, but I trust God to continue to lead me deeper as I lead them into a well-rooted faith. Eventually, they might end up leading me as well.

· · · · · · · · KEY POINTS · · · · · · · ·

- There are pros and cons to behaviors becoming automatic habits. It's amazing that we're doing it, but our habits can also become rote or legalistic.

- The solution to habits becoming rote is to change them up and deepen them.

- To deepen a habit, we can make it longer, make it more complex, or attach another habit.

· · · · · · · · · YOUR TURN · · · · · · · ·

1. What faith habit in your life is starting to feel a little dry and stagnant?

   _____

   _____

2. How could you deepen or modify the habit by making it longer or more complex, or by attaching another habit?

   _____

   _____

3. What is a current faith struggle in your family? Where will you look for a resource to help with that specific struggle?

   _____

   _____

4. What is one thing you want to remember from this chapter?

   _____

   _____

MELISSA'S STORY

I've always prayed with my kids before bed, but one night when I was praying with them, I decided to end with the Lord's Prayer like my church did when I was growing up: "We ask all these things in Jesus' name, who taught us to pray, 'Our Father, who art in heaven . . .'" I thought it would be a good prayer to teach them and that if we said it together every night, they would probably memorize it easily. Since we were already in the habit of praying every night, it was an easy addition to our usual prayers.

At first, I just started saying that prayer on my own at the end of our prayers. But after hearing it several times, my three-year-old son memorized it and started saying it with me, and then he began asking if he could lead that part of the prayer instead. Soon afterward, his two-year-old sister was trying to say it along with us too, and she eventually memorized the whole thing as well. Even though I knew they didn't fully understand what all the words meant yet, I also knew they would understand more as they grew older and that it would be a good bit of Scripture to have in their heads and their hearts.

My kids are now five and six, and we still end our nightly prayers with the Lord's Prayer. Sometimes they pray it aloud with me and sometimes they don't. But even though they don't always say it with me anymore, I think having that prayer in their memories helped my kids get more comfortable praying aloud. My son and daughter now pray out loud at night, for our blessings before meals, and occasionally when other situations call for prayer (like when someone gets hurt or they are upset or happy about something). We have also had many occasions to talk through the meaning of the Lord's Prayer over the years or to refer to it when teaching other lessons. And it helps unify us in our prayer time when we all end with that prayer each night. Even when they don't say it out loud with me, I can tell they're usually praying along.[3]

MELISSA FAULKNER

HOW DO I GET THEM TO DO IT ALONE?

Preparing Our Kids to Own Their Faith

A FEW YEARS AGO, I wanted my kids to move toward greater ownership of their faith practices, but I also knew (a) my kids were young, (b) God had my children in his hands, and therefore (c) I didn't have to panic. The all-out team was loudly calling me over, but I chose to step into the freedom of the bit-by-bit team instead.

First, I took stock of what was already happening in my family. My kids, even at a young age, were getting to know God through his Word because we read the Bible together in the mornings. But I wanted to give them a step toward independence. That's when I decided to revisit the Faith Growth Cycle:

- **Seed Stage:** I knew I wanted to move our kids intentionally and incrementally toward faith practices that they could do on their own—and might serve as the foundation for their own lifelong relationships with God. Growing into individual friendships with him would bring glory to him. So I prayed about what God wanted to do with our family to move us toward something where our kids could be more independent and engaged.

I also needed to examine my obstacles. I wanted to invite them to read the Bible themselves, but it takes longer to help my kids look up and read Bible passages than it does to just do it myself. I was also worried that my kids wouldn't be able to read all the words or that they'd all want to read the passage and I'd have to break up a fight. In general, my obstacle was my own impatience.

- **Sprout Stage:** With my vision and obstacles in mind, I decided on a small step forward. Instead of me looking up the passage and reading it aloud, I could attach a new habit onto my original family Bible reading practice: I would have them all look up the Bible verse with me and read it aloud to each other. It was a small step—but one step closer to them taking responsibility for their own faith.

  Since we were already used to reading the Bible in the mornings together, the new little habit was just to ask them to open their own Bibles and find the passage. I made sure it was easy to implement by storing three children's Bibles in the kitchen.

- **Root Stage:** To make this habit more meaningful, we spent a few weeks that spring watching the Buck Denver Asks . . . What's in the Bible? series of videos,[1] which gave them an overview of what is in the Bible and where to find things.

Over the past years, my kids have become much more biblically literate simply by opening their own Bibles. It seems obvious, but it was the right little step for us, and I needed this step-by-step approach to help me move past my obstacles. A couple of years later, I decided to take this up a notch and see what would happen if I asked my kids to read that day's Bible passage on their own at breakfast time *before* I joined them at the table. We talk about it once everyone has read it, and I invite them to share things they noticed or questioned about the passage. The transition hasn't been easy—they sometimes don't eat breakfast until I show up, or they "forget" (meaning they do something more fun while they eat, then claim to forget)—but I'm playing the long game here and not giving in to fear when they forget (accidentally or on purpose) to read before we meet.

INDEPENDENT ROOTS

Encouraging our kids to be more independent in their faith is one more way to deeply root any current habit. Kids love to feel grown-up and independent, and we can use that natural tendency to empower them to take ownership of their faith journey.

Because we all long to see our kids choosing to build their own relationship with God, we can tend to see spiritual independence as an "all or nothing" moment. We pass our nine-year-old a devotional or our middle schooler a Bible study, wipe our hands in satisfaction, and call it independence. However, becoming independent at anything takes more than just being handed the tools. If I were a journeyman carpenter, I wouldn't just hand my new apprentice a hammer and shoo them away to build a cabinet. The apprentice would first watch, then participate, then be given small jobs with basic tools. As they proved themselves competent, they'd be given more responsibility with more access to power tools. This process takes years, as does moving our kids into deeper spiritual independence. However, that doesn't mean we can't start the process when they're young! Moving our kids into deeper independence can occur at any stage in their development.

Let's look at what moving toward independence looks like at different stages of development.

- **Toddler/Preschool:** In this stage, kids tend to be mostly dependent on us because we're reading to them, teaching prayers, and turning on music. However, there are some small steps we can take to help them move toward independence, particularly with prayer:
  - Instead of the parent always choosing what will be taught that day, invite your child to choose a favorite Christian picture book or Bible story to read, or ask them to suggest a favorite song.
  - During prayer, ask your child to thank God for things they love.
  - Create a prayer journal with space to draw their prayers.
  - Teach your child a simple prayer pattern to fill in on their own, such as, *God, today I liked* _____, *and today I didn't like* _____.
  - Give your child the chance to speak from their own heart during prayer time.

- **Early Elementary:** At this stage, most kids will want to start doing some things on their own. Follow your child's cues, but you can also start encouraging some small steps toward independence in Scripture reading as well as a more personal prayer life:
  - As your child learns to read, ask them to pick out words they recognize in your devotional or Bible reading.
  - If you're reading a devotional together, invite your early reader to read part of it, like the beginning Scripture or the ending prayer.
  - Give your child an easy-to-read Bible translation (I suggest the NIrV for this age and the NLT for older elementary kids).
  - Ask your child to read a section of the Bible before you discuss it as a family.
  - Give your child Bible-based books they can read on their own (such as the children's Bible books from Kaleidoscope or a graphic novel version of the Bible).
  - Help your child learn the words to the songs sung in church so they can participate on Sundays.
  - Give your child a fun-looking journal, inviting them to write down prayers or copy out favorite Bible verses.
  - Invite your child to listen for God's words or nudges in their heart.

- **Later Elementary (and Beyond):** During these years, we need to pay close attention to our child's interest in spiritual things, learning when we need to push them a bit harder and when we need to continue to do the faith practices alongside them. Some kids will be ready for an independent Bible study at age ten because they naturally have a hunger for more of God. Others will appear uninterested until their later teen years. This is a stage for building confidence in the spiritual disciplines, but you'll also need to pray that your child *wants* to do them because it's at this point where kids can start to resent our faith-building efforts. Philippians 2:13 reminds us that "God is working in you, giving you the desire and the power to do what pleases him." As you are encouraging your child toward more independence in their faith journey, pray that God gives them the desire! Here are some ideas for slowly nudging your older kids deeper:

- Ask your child to read the Bible passage aloud.
- Ask your child to pray out loud or lead in prayer.
- Invite an interested child to create a devotional for younger siblings.
- Work with an older child to set their own faith goals (like reading through the New Testament, raising money for an orphanage, or fasting from video games).
- Invite them to use digital faith tools like the Kids Bible Experience or the Lectio for Families app. There are many other Bible-based apps springing up all the time, and digital tools can make the difference between resistance and engagement.
- Offer interesting Bible study aids to help keep their interest up, such as videos from BibleProject, reading plans through the YouVersion Bible App, or podcasts like *The Bible Recap*.

None of these seem like they will make that much of a difference on their own, but just as we discovered with the Sprout Stage, the small things matter deeply. Each progressive step provides a little more independence, leading to a child who fully takes the reins of their own relationship with God.

FROM PARTNERSHIP TO OWNERSHIP

A podcast host once asked me how to get kids to do their own devotions. Since we were already in the middle of recording, I felt cornered and guilty. How could I answer? My kids weren't doing their own, and I bumbled around so much that the host contacted me a few days later, apologized for putting me on the spot, and offered to re-record that portion of the interview. Thankfully, I was able to move out of that crisis moment quickly because I had discovered how to harness the power of small habits to make big changes that could help my kids move into a more independent stage, which I was able to share when we re-recorded.

My vision: I wanted my son to grow a personal relationship with God, not one that's dependent on me. Thus far we had only done faith practices in partnership, but I wanted him to learn how to take ownership of his faith journey. However, I didn't want to just chuck a devotional at my twelve-year-old and leave it all up to him.

My obstacle: I didn't know how to lead him toward ownership without making it seem like a chore for him. So I prayed about it, and God helped me figure out a little habit that would help my son.

First, we talked about why he should read the Bible on his own. Then, together, we figured out a good time. Our original plan was that he'd read a small section of the Bible when he finished brushing his teeth at night. But for at least a year, his unofficial prompt became the moment I called up the stairs, "Hey, are you ready for me?" The conversation itself became a reward for him, because if he didn't read the Bible, he just received a quick blessing and a kiss good night.

Once that became a habit, I let him pick out a new journal. I invited him to write down something small each time he reads his Bible. It could be a verse he read, a question for God, or a short prayer. He's not a long-winded writer, but sometimes he's shown me prayers he's been inspired to pray, or even a poem or psalm of his own. I'm sure that some days this feels rote to him, just like journaling or Bible study sometimes feels like a slog to me. But over time, he'll discover that as he opens up that time for God to speak, God will sometimes surprise him! Over the past two and a half years, he's read the whole New Testament and most of the Old Testament. When he starts a new book of the Bible, he asks me to pull up an overview video from BibleProject, and we watch it together. He's beginning to dig deeper with some study material like *The Bible Recap* by Tara-Leigh Cobble, and his personal Bible study continues to open interesting doors for conversation between the two of us—and sometimes the whole family!

I can also see his choices and behavior becoming more Christlike—not because I'm forcing compliance but because he's being formed by the Spirit of Christ inside him. Over the past few years, he's moved from a place where I was directing his faith habits into a place where he's mostly in charge. Because we're used to walking our faith lives together, I still get to be the first place he goes when he has faith struggles or questions.

This slow, bit-by-bit process leads our kids to feel ownership over their faith practices without dissociating completely from the family faith practices they grew up with. In the end, we don't want kids who are so independent that they become disconnected, never talking to us anymore. We want them to think for themselves and take responsibility for their relationship with God, but we also want them to continue to talk with us when they have questions or doubts. We want our teens and adult children to continue to trust us with their prayer requests, to discuss where they think God is leading them, to let us keep texting them biblical encouragement (and to send us encouragements of their own), and to share their questions and discoveries. I believe that *interdependence*, rather than complete *independence*, is the goal of our spiritual parenting efforts and prayers. As we lead our kids on a bit-by-bit journey of spiritual ownership, we're moving toward a more relationally connected long-term goal: raising kids who still love to interdependently connect with us spiritually.

KEY POINTS

- Spiritual independence isn't a single moment, but a long process of equipping our kids to take ownership over their relationship with God.

- Each progressive step provides a little more ownership, leading a child to fully take the reins of their own relationship with God.

- As we lead our kids on a bit-by-bit journey of independence, we're moving toward a more relationally connected long-term goal: raising kids who still love to interdependently connect with us spiritually.

· · · · · · · · · · YOUR TURN · · · · · · · · ·

1. What does independence look like for your kids in the stage(s) they're in?

    _____

    _____

2. What small step could you take to encourage your child toward deeper ownership of their faith journey?

    _____

    _____

3. If your child is a teen, how can you foster ownership while still encouraging an interdependent relationship where you grow spiritually, together?

    _____

    _____

4. What is one thing you want to remember from this chapter?

    _____

    _____

RUTH'S STORY

I was a bit apprehensive when we put our habit recipe together—I wasn't sure that we would remember to do it, or that my kids would join in. I also wasn't sure if it would be enough and if I should be doing more.

However, remembering was much easier than I'd thought. Tying it to something we do every day, like eating, meant that we didn't forget to read our Bible verse (because we didn't forget to eat!). We haven't chosen to stay with the habit in the form we started it, however, because we tried out some changes that made it work better. What doing the habit recipe did was help me move on from beating myself up for doing nothing. I had to start somewhere. It was a really good start, even if it didn't work long term, because it showed me that I could take small steps. Our first habit wasn't as hard as I'd thought it would be, and my kids were less negative than I'd anticipated, while still letting me know that things didn't work for them.

So why aren't we still doing it if it was so helpful? First, starting the habit as a family made me realize that doing something with all three of my kids (ages seven, three, and eighteen months) didn't work well. But it made us talk about what we could do. My eldest has been getting good with independent reading, so we've found him some Bible and devotional books he enjoys. He reads some and we chat about it. My middle child is more interested in prayer and learning to talk to God, so we're learning some prayers she can say. My youngest tends to just charge about while we're doing this, so I'm working on adding a new habit of praying a blessing over her each day.[2]

RUTH HANCOCK

WHAT DO I DO WHEN LIFE CHANGES?

Re-cycling the Cycle of Faith Growth

"Hey, Mom," my preschooler pipes up. Summer sweat trickles down my brow as I scurry around the kitchen, tidying up in the middle of another long summer day.

"Yeah, bud?" I say, distractedly shoving a piece of paper into the recycle bin.

"Remember when we used to read the Bible at breakfast? We should do that again."

I stop and gape at him, shocked that he noticed the inevitable *summer slide*.

I planned for us to get back to our morning routine when September rolled around again, but he was just a little guy, not understanding the difference between the school year and summer, wondering why we weren't doing what we used to do.

Sometimes—or a lot of times—we're going to encounter fresh obstacles along our family discipleship journey, especially when our anchor prompts vanish. Summer holidays arrive, and "when I'm waiting for the bus" is no longer a good anchor for your Bible memory habit. You suddenly realize you haven't tucked in your teenager this whole week, which means you didn't get to pray with him. You started working evenings, which means you're not snuggling with your preschoolers and blessing them as they drift off to sleep. Soccer season arrives and you spend more time in the car than at the dinner table, so your hard-won nightly Bible reading habit goes out the window.

New obstacles can also pop up as our kids grow and have different needs than they did when they were younger. You might notice your daughter having a lot of questions that could be solved if you took the time to dig into apologetics with her. Maybe your son needs to have consistent, open conversations about sexuality, or your child has recurring issues with a kid at school.

Change itself isn't an obstacle, though. It's an opportunity.

To return to our garden metaphor, now that I've learned how to choose the right seeds for my garden, plant them in straight rows, and give them the unique care they need to grow deep roots, I can use what I've learned to nourish the plants, not just for a single season but for a lifetime. After all, different seasons and years require different approaches, even for the same plants! If I plant zucchini in the same spot in my garden every year, the zucchini plants will become less fruitful because they are huge plants that sap all the nutrients from the area. I need to plant them in a different place that still has lots of nutrients. Just as crops need to be rotated annually for continued fruitfulness, we should be watchful for when a new parenting season requires adjusting a habit or approach. As life shifts and changes, I need to know how to shift and modify my family's faith habits so they become beautiful, embedded rhythms of faith that can adapt to whatever stage my child is at—and stand the test of time.

So how do you navigate those big and small shifts without losing steam or giving up? How do you address the new needs that emerge?

RE-CYCLE THE CYCLE

Instead of getting discouraged or frustrated, you just go through the Faith Growth Cycle again. When you encounter a disruption to your family's schedule or realize you're in a new life stage, go straight back to the Seed Stage and talk to God about your family's obstacles and needs. Find a new habit and anchor in the Sprout Stage. Once that habit is working for your family, go deeper in the Root Stage.

Going through the Faith Growth Cycle again doesn't mean you've failed or are starting all over—it simply means your family needs to assess what's happening. You're not going backward; you're giving yourself permission to reset, make things simple, and adapt to whatever your family's needs are.

For example, a child moving from the toddler to the preschool stage is now able to speak clearly and memorize quickly. When you talk to God about your child's new needs and your family's current obstacles, you may realize that your child is ready for Bible memory verses or a more robust prayer life. Choose a small new habit and anchor, and you'll find your child growing deeper with God.

Or perhaps your kids have started to play a sport, and you find yourself in the car most evenings and weekends. This rushed lifestyle does not have to stop you from discipling them. In fact, these drives can become the perfect moments to listen to worship music or a Bible-based podcast, pray together, or talk about what's going on in their lives. Have a chat with God about the best way forward in this season, and then start with something small. The family car becomes the kitchen table, and even better, you have a captive crowd!

We can learn how to use the Seed, Sprout, and Root Stages as a cycle to partner with God for our child's spiritual growth in every season, all the way to the season in which their spiritual growth journey becomes their own. You can even teach your kids how to use the Faith Growth Cycle, so when your child moves away from home, they'll already have the tools to establish their own habit of meeting with God or to think through how to consistently get to church.

The Faith Growth Cycle is a simple method you can use over and over as your family grows up, allowing you to flourish spiritually. Using the Faith Growth Cycle as a paradigm for habit change will help you think through what your family needs in each season, as well as have the conversations with God that need to happen all the time as you raise kids.

WHAT DOES FLOURISHING LOOK LIKE?

Just like a tree can be healthy and flourishing at many stages of life, spiritual flourishing isn't an end point. Rather, a flourishing family is one living in a place of dependence on God—a place where each member is being formed into a Kingdom person in age-appropriate ways. A family can flourish in any season:

- In the toddler years, *flourishing* simply means your child learns to trust God because they've learned to trust you as their caregiver. When you say "God loves you" to them, they believe it because your loving arms are holding them.

- In the preschool years, *flourishing* might look like a family who playacts Bible stories every night, belly laughing over kids pretending to be terrifying angels. Or it might look like children who see their dad reading his Bible on the couch each morning, inviting them to snuggle and read with him when they bounce out of bed far earlier than he would like. It might look like a child dancing to worship music in the kitchen as Mom praises God while wiping counters. It's tempting to think that some of these situations are holier than others or more formative for your children than others. But in the end, God will work with your personality and your unique family, bringing you to a place of spiritual flourishing that looks uniquely like *you*.

- *Flourishing* in the younger school years might look like a family who loves reading the Bible together at the dinner table, having debates and conversations about Bible translations. But it could also look like quiet prayers together at bedtime, a robust Bible memory program, or a morning devotional podcast in the car. It might even look like opening up your home to a Bible college student or bringing baked goods to the food bank on a regular basis. Remember, you don't need to do it all or know it all to make a difference in your child's faith. You just need to follow God's lead and start small.

- In the teen years, *flourishing* looks even more diverse. Your teen's faith might be forming mostly in the middle of the night as they pray through their anxiety, in the locker room as they learn to stand up for a vulnerable student, or at a church Bible study—while your role becomes that of a cheerleader and resource finder. But as you're consistent in praying for guidance and implementing small habits, you will see flourishing happening in different ways. It may not always be the way you expect or hope for, but you will see growth. Relationship breakthroughs will happen, and you'll have conversations that wouldn't have occurred without your intentional faith practices.

The apostle Paul shared with us his vision for flourishing faith:

> Work hard to show the results of your salvation, obeying God with deep reverence and fear. For God is working in you, giving you the desire and the power to do what pleases him.
>
> Do everything without complaining and arguing, so that no one can criticize you. Live clean, innocent lives as children of God, shining like bright lights in a world full of crooked and perverse people.
>
> PHILIPPIANS 2:12-15

You can live out this vision in any season of life. Your family can spiritually flourish in the toddler stage, with preschoolers, middle schoolers, teens, and as adults, becoming bright lights in a world of darkness and pain.

As you learn to apply the Faith Growth Cycle to new situations and continue to grow faith rhythms that fit your unique family, you'll help your child grow in independence and confidence so they can move into a faith that is their own. None of you will ever arrive at perfect spirituality, but you'll thrive in this place where you're consistently inviting God to work in your life and responding with obedience.

I once heard a Tanzanian proverb that reminds me to parent in light of this long game: "Little by little, a little becomes a lot." We're forming little habits to address the needs of the moment, but we do so knowing that we are slowly nurturing a deeply rooted faith that, as God works in our child's life, may grow fruit in his timing.

We can't force our kids to grow a relationship with God, and we can't make their hearts soft. But by the grace of God, we can be intentional about discipling our kids—trusting that with God, little by little, a little becomes a lot and leads to flourishing family faith.

KEY POINTS

- The Faith Growth Cycle can be reused at many different times in life. It becomes the simple, step-by-step process you can use whenever God calls you or your child to go deeper in your relationship with him.

- Spiritual flourishing isn't an end point, but it looks different at various stages and will be unique to your family.

- Little by little, a little becomes a lot and leads to flourishing family faith.

YOUR TURN

1. What is currently changing (or about to change) in your family's schedule?

_____

_____

2. How can you use the Faith Growth Cycle to rework your family's faith habits for the current (or upcoming) situation?

_____

_____

3. Where do you see God working in your family members' spiritual lives right now?

_____

_____

4. What is one thing you want to remember from this chapter?

_____

_____

DIANE'S STORY

My habit plan was to practice a memory verse in the car with my granddaughter right after we fastened our seat belts. It was so simple, I was pretty sure she would like it, but I wasn't sure it would make much of an impact. I also wasn't confident I would keep up with it—I am not good at sticking to habits even when it is something important to me.

This habit, though, turned out to be an awesome way for us to start the day: focused on God's Word and on a positive note. Our day often started as a struggle due to my granddaughter's anxiety. When I offered to pray for her, she would say no, but she was more open to saying a Scripture verse together.

We started by memorizing 2 Corinthians 5:17 from a Bible study we'd been going through on who we are in Christ. After we had the verse memorized, we talked about what it meant. Later, when we started home-schooling, we transitioned to doing a Bible study right after breakfast. Practicing that one verse in the car was a great way to introduce the verse first, and because it was part of our routine, she didn't balk at doing more. Talking about God's Word wasn't something extra; it was just what we did on the way to school. I later asked her if she remembers that habit, and she remembered the verses we had memorized almost word for word. When I asked her if it was helpful, she told me, "It helped me relax and brace myself for the day ahead."[1]

DIANE UNGER

FINAL THOUGHTS

IF YOU READ THROUGH THE BIBLE with an eye toward the small, you'll discover many flabbergasting ways that God takes a willing person with many flaws and weaknesses and flows through that person to share his goodness and glory. David was a simple shepherd boy with a heart for God, and God worked through him to bind together the nation of Israel and start the lineage of kings that led to Jesus. Ruth was a foreign widow who simply offered her heart to her mother-in-law. Through her, God showed an incredible picture of redemption—and brought this foreigner into the household of the Messiah. Mary was a teenager who said yes to bringing God himself into the world. Priscilla and Aquila were a Roman Jewish couple who ran a tent-making business, and God worked through both of them to teach and grow the early church.

Time and again the Bible shows us ordinary, broken people whom God worked in and through to bring his plans to pass. If God can work through cowards like Moses, uneducated fishermen like Peter and John, teenage mothers like Mary, and wives like Priscilla, he can work through you.

Through the power of the Holy Spirit, you can share your real (and growing) faith with your kids. You can teach them the basics of the Christian faith so they have a foundation upon which to grow. You can instill faith practices that will help them connect with God for a lifetime. You can plant seeds of faith simply by living your own faith in front of them. And just as importantly, you can do this all within a loving (although not perfect) relationship.

You can't give your children new hearts, but you can point them to the one who can. The path to a flourishing faith is not about being perfect or having all the answers. It's about pointing our children to Jesus and trusting him with the rest.

I want to leave you with one last thought: *You are not alone.* Family discipleship can feel overwhelming at times, but know that God is with you every step of the way. Lean on him for wisdom and strength, and don't be afraid to ask other believers in your community for help. After all, "one of the most effective things you can do to build better habits is to join a culture where your desired behavior is the normal behavior."[1] When we try to do faith on our own, we become like a coal removed from a fire pit but expected to remain red-hot. It's tough to stay passionate when we're all alone. Lean on God, find your people, start small, and go with this blessing:

May the Lord bless you and keep you,
May the Lord make his face shine on you and be gracious
    to you;
May the Lord turn his face toward you and give you peace.

Growing with you,
Christie

JENNIFER'S STORY

When Christie first helped me put together the habit recipe, I initially didn't even know what habit to implement. None of the options seemed doable for our family, and I honestly didn't think that we would stick to any of them. Anytime I tried to implement something in the past, we would either give up after a few days, or worse, not even make it through the first day. I've had countless experiences preparing plans and printing activities only to give up before even starting because I could never find the "right" time to start.

This time, though, Christie proposed some simple ideas to start with, and as we communicated, the Holy Spirit led me to pursue praying over my kids before they left the house every morning. It seemed simple enough, so we made a plan. Going into the first day, I was not optimistic that it would last. My kids are troupers, and they typically go along with the ideas I come up with, so no one complained, and we got through day one without any trouble. I just hoped we could continue on with it. And to my surprise, we did. Having a "trigger" to help me remember has been key to making this work.

As my kids grab their backpacks to head to school, we pray before they leave. My kids have taken ownership of the activity, and there have been a few days when my daughter has reminded me that we needed to pray before they left. We have not been perfect at it, and we have missed a day or two here and there, but overall, we have kept up with this habit. Early on, I did have one morning when I basically yelled a prayer over them as they got out of the car at school drop-off, but other than that, we have been fairly consistent at praying before leaving the house.

Before this new habit, we already prayed over meals and at bedtime, but starting our day with prayer has been a good reminder for the whole family to pause during the most hectic part of our day to refocus on God and his will for our day. What initially started with just me praying over the family has led to my kids asking to take turns to pray over us, which has been a blessing for me to see.

We have continued with this habit for several months now, and I am confident that we will be able to continue it for years to come.[2]

JENNIFER ZIMMERMAN

Appendix A

IDEAS FOR LITTLE HABITS

STARTING A LITTLE FAITH HABIT with your family can feel daunting! You may have already landed on an idea, but if you need inspiration, this list is a great jumping-off point. Don't choose something that you feel you *should* do. Choose one behavior that you actually want to do and think would be easy! When you start with a habit that will bring you joy, you're more likely to remember and continue it. Don't forget: "First steps always seem like not enough, but they are the bravest and they start the journey to where you're meant to go. It takes great trust to believe in the smallness of beginnings."[1]

LITTLE PRAYER HABITS

- Say the Lord's Prayer (or another short, memorized prayer) together.

- Pray for your child.
- Focus on one kind of prayer (praise, thanksgiving, confession, or petition).
- Stretch and say, "Thank you, God, for this day."
- Thank God for the meal you're about to eat.
- Thank God for the meal you just ate.
- Say a short prayer of gratitude.
- Say a short prayer for someone you love.
- See who can come up with the most things to thank God for.
- Ask your child to fill in the blanks: *God, today I liked* _____, *and God, today I didn't like* _____.
- Pray for the parent or caregiver who just left for work or to run errands.
- Go on a prayer walk in your neighborhood and pray for your neighbors.
- Say the Jesus prayer while slowly breathing in and out. (In: "Lord Jesus Christ" Out: "Have mercy on me.")

LITTLE SCRIPTURE HABITS

- Speak a Bible verse blessing over your child (the same one every day).
- Read one Bible verse and ask, "What does this show us about God?"
- Ask, "Does this remind you of anything from the Bible?"
- When you pass a Scripture verse posted in your home, read it out loud.
- Sit on the couch and read the Bible for thirty seconds, out loud, with no expectation that anyone will listen.
- Read a *short* devotion.

- Recite a memory verse aloud.
- Hang a verse on your fridge and say it together, once per day.
- Turn on an audio Bible.
- Invite your child to read their Bible alongside you.

LITTLE WORSHIP HABITS

- Say, "Be the center of our day, Jesus."
- Turn on Christian music in the background.
- Turn on a Christian worship playlist on YouTube instead of a show.
- Sing hymns while you cook dinner.
- Point to something in nature and say, "God created that! Isn't he an amazing artist/builder/scientist?"
- Light a candle to remind you that Jesus is the light of the world.
- Make the sign of the cross.
- Sing a worship song.
- Read a one-page biography of a faith hero.
- Read a Christian picture book.
- Twirl your child and say, "God made you and loves you so much!"
- Hug your child and say, "I love you, and God loves you even more."
- Set aside money for giving to others.
- Choose an item for the food bank.
- Choose a special treat only for Sundays.

THE BLESSING HABIT

ONE OF OUR BOYS STRUGGLED with anxiety when he was younger. Social anxiety, school anxiety, separation anxiety—you name it, he wrestled with it. I am not a worrier, so sometimes it's hard for me to identify with him. I want to say, "Well, that's silly. That probably won't happen!" I learned the hard way that a flippant response doesn't help.

When he was in kindergarten, he struggled so much with separation, gym class, writing, and friends. I started praying a blessing over him in April, and in June it occurred to me that his anxieties had almost completely lifted. They weren't entirely gone, so we continued to pray the same blessing over him nightly.

One night, when he experienced a deep bout of anxiety, I prayed for ideas to help my little man. And just like that, I was suddenly reminded of the blessing we had been praying over him daily for the past nine months. God nudged me to realize that this blessing was more than a prayer: It was also instructions.

> Don't worry about anything; instead, *pray about everything. Tell God what you need,* and *thank him for all he has done.* Then you will experience God's peace, which exceeds anything we can understand. His peace will guard your hearts and minds as you live in Christ Jesus.
>
> PHILIPPIANS 4:6-7, EMPHASIS ADDED

I lifted my sweet boy onto my lap (not an easy feat with a seven-year-old whose cozy squish had turned into sharp elbows and knees) and reminded him of the verse. Then we did what the verse told us to do.

First, we prayed. I prayed for him, then he prayed.

Second, we told God what he needed: peace.

Third, we thanked God for all he had done. We thanked God for family. We named all his friends. We remembered the special toys, puzzles, and games in his life. We were thankful for his teacher, his brothers, and the food he ate.

At that point, he was still upset, so we did it all again. Finally, my boy calmed down and realized how exhausted he was. I tucked him into bed and commissioned him to keep thinking of all the things God had done for him until he fell asleep.

As I've continued to pray this blessing over him every night for years, I've watched his worries hold less tightly. And when they do start to cling again, it doesn't take much more than a few words for us to be reminded of God's command to pray and give thanks as well as God's precious promise to guard his heart and mind. As he's grown, he's become far bolder than I would have expected, and he's told me of multiple times he invited God into his worries, even without me reminding him.

I've taught this specific twenty-second-per-day habit to others for over fifteen years (since before my oldest child was even born), and I have seen the astounding long-term impact it has on other families as well. I've heard of kids falling asleep better and no longer having nightmares. I've heard of children with learning disabilities memorizing and applying Scripture. And many families have grown from this tiny habit to a full-on Bible study time.

WHAT IS A BIBLICAL BLESSING?

Praying a nightly prayer of blessing over your child is the simplest habit you could ever start.

Because it's so simple, it's not hard to push through the first-time awkwardness.

Because it's so simple, it easily becomes part of your bedtime routine.

Because it's so simple, you can do it even when you're tired, sick, or away from home.

Because it's so simple, you and your kids will accidentally memorize Scripture.

Sounds wonderful, right? It gets even better. In Deuteronomy, we read Moses' encouragement to the people of Israel:

> "This day I call the heavens and the earth as witnesses against you that I have set before you life and death, blessings and curses. Now choose life, so that you and

your children may live and that you may love the LORD
your God, listen to his voice, and hold fast to him."

DEUTERONOMY 30:19-20, NIV

What exactly are blessings and curses, anyway? In *The
Blessing*, authors John Trent, Gary Smalley, and Kari Trent
Stageberg dive into the Hebrew words for *blessing* and *curse*,
offering two helpful definitions:

1. Blessing someone essentially tells them: "You are of such
   great value to me, I choose to add to your life."[1] This
   is what dads in the Old Testament often did for their
   children (most obviously seen in the stories of Isaac and
   Jacob, recorded in Genesis 27 and 49, respectively), and
   Paul did this in all his letters.

2. On the other hand, "the word for *curse* in this
   Deuteronomy passage literally means a 'trickle' or 'muddy
   stream' caused by a dam or obstruction upstream. For
   [the Hebrews], living in desert lands, cutting off water
   meant cutting off life itself. So do you get the terrible
   word picture here? When we curse someone, we are
   choosing to 'dam up the stream' on life-giving actions
   and words that could flow down to that person."[2]

Blessing and cursing our children can take place on many
levels, as we all know. The way we talk to and treat our children
daily can be a blessing or a curse. But I've seen that the verbal
biblical blessing is the quickest, easiest way to have a positive
impact.

One of the best-known biblical blessings is often called the *priestly blessing* because the priests were to speak it over the people of Israel:

> The LORD said to Moses, "Tell Aaron and his sons, 'This is how you are to bless the Israelites. Say to them:
>
>> """The LORD bless you
>>   and keep you;
>> the LORD make his face shine on you
>>   and be gracious to you;
>> the LORD turn his face toward you
>>   and give you peace.""""
>
> NUMBERS 6:22-26, NIV

As we can see from the repetition of "the LORD," the key to the biblical blessing is God. Biblical blessings are not generic blessings of peace, happiness, and success on your child's life, nor are they something you wish for your child's future. Those kinds of affirmations are lovely sentiments, but they lack the power of praying Scripture over your child. Blessing your child passes on the Lord God's blessings to them. It declares God's truth over your child's life. A blessing is not me saying, "This is what I would like to see in your life" or even "Here's a thing I like about you." A biblical blessing is God saying, "This is what I want to do with your life."

Here's how to bless your child: Take twenty seconds per night to put your hand on your child's head, look them in the eye, and speak the words of God over them.

Psalm 139:5 says that God places "[his] hand of blessing on my head." Appropriate touch can be so meaningful, especially after a hard day with the kids. When the *last* thing you want to do is touch your children gently, placing a gentle hand on them and blessing them is the way to release the built-up pressure from the day.

In Ephesians 4:26 we are told, "Don't let the sun go down while you are still angry." It's so important for my children to know that they can lie down and sleep in peace because I've gently blessed them even after an aggravating day. You can use the same blessing every day for your child, or you can choose different verses for different children or pick a new verse when a new need arises. Don't let that little voice in your head tell you that it's a waste of time or that it's too awkward. Use what you've learned about starting new habits and try it out tonight.

GOD'S NAME FOR YOUR CHILD

When I was in third grade, a boy called me Bossy. In sixth grade, teachers called me Quiet. When I was in junior high, boys called me Ugly and girls called me Shy. And in high school, a parent called me Critical. These are all names that have been put on me at some point in my life.

Names are powerful. We've all had names given to us and put on us. Think back to your childhood and the names your parents, teachers, and peers gave you. What names come to mind? Some may be innocent pet names, others may make you cringe, and still others may have caused lifelong pain.

But of course, the name-calling hasn't stopped with us. Just like the world labeled us when we were kids, it will label our kids. The world thrives on putting people into neat, labeled boxes categorized by ethnicity, sexuality, personality, or religion. Our children will get names from peers, teachers, random people on the internet—and even from us.

What names do your children already carry? Is your son The One with ADHD? Is your daughter The Quiet One? Is your child The Sensitive One, The Annoying One, The Strong-Willed One? The Chatterbox, The Cute One, The Talented One, The Needy One?

It took me years to get over the names people had spoken over me, the curses people had unintentionally given me. If a curse is like a dam built up to block the life-giving words from getting through, each of those people in my life had taken a rock, put a name on it, and placed it in that dam. God had to remove those rocks one by one to allow his life-giving water to flow again.

But when I finally came to the realization that I am the Lord's and no one else's and that he loves me with an everlasting love, he gave me a new name: a name that shows how my life and my future are so connected to him. Yahweh, the God Who Was and Is and Is to Come, has put his name on me, washing away those rocks of cursing with the river of blessing.

In Numbers 6:27, God tells Moses why the priests are to bless the Israelites: "They will put my name on the Israelites, and I will bless them" (NIV). Just like the nations around Israel knew the Israelites were The People of Yahweh, your child can be known as The Child of Yahweh. Isn't that an infinitely better name than all the others?

Think again of those names you were called in your youth. Some of them have likely defined you, maybe even changed you, for good or for bad. In my pivotal third-grade moment, I was taking charge of a group project, and this boy was annoyed . . . so he called me Bossy. Years later, I realized that at that moment, I had shrunk back—and I'd ended up squelching my leadership skills for many years. Had I known that my third-grade "bossiness" was a gift from God in disguise, I might be further along in becoming who God created me to be.

In blessing your children day in and day out, you can help your children know and live out of their true name as you put God's name on them. Revelation 22:4 says that believers "will see [God's] face, and his name will be written on their foreheads." I want God's name to be written on the foreheads of all my sons in permanent ink. Praying the priestly blessing over your children is one of the ways you can show them the goodness of God—and help them remove the rocks of cursing they'll encounter. As we speak God's blessings over our kids, the river of his life-giving water flows forth so they may live freely in the way God created them.

Some might say that God's blessing looks like a healthy family, a satisfying job, and enough money to spare. But God's blessing looks like a child who loves the Lord, listens to his voice, and holds fast to him. A child who follows God like that will also grow in the fruit of love, joy, peace, patience, kindness, goodness, faithfulness, gentleness, and self-control! That child will desire to connect with God daily, repent of sins, and let Jesus be the Lord of their life. I'm convinced that if God blesses my children to love the Lord, listen to his voice, and hold fast to him, the world won't be able to throw anything at them they can't handle—because they'll be walking with God the whole time.

THE BLESSING RIPPLE EFFECT

I taught a class on blessings annually in my church for ten years, have spoken about it at other churches and homeschool conferences, and created an email class that about two thousand people went through. As a result, I've been privileged to see many families changed in huge ways because of this one simple habit! One consistent impact is this: The blessing habit creates space, motivation, and excitement for going deeper in other family faith habits. The following are stories from my family and others that show what God can do through such a simple habit.

More Scripture Memory

Janet and Kevin[3] have multiple adopted children, some of whom deal with fetal alcohol spectrum disorders (FASD), permanent brain damage caused by alcohol during pregnancy. These kids' brains are changed in a way that makes it hard for them to retain information, which means they struggle with memorization. However, Janet and Kevin have been so faithfully praying Joshua 1:9 over their kids that each one has memorized this verse! How significant and incredible it is that they know the Lord their God will be with them wherever they go.

Janet and Kevin's six-year-old was born addicted to cocaine and has a severe FASD. Brain scans have revealed heartbreaking amounts of brain damage. According to doctors, he was never supposed to be able to synthesize and apply information. But he's now memorized two verses and preaches them to his sisters at appropriate times! This keystone habit created a structure in his life and in his brain, and he was able to not only memorize two verses that his mom prayed over him but also apply them. His mom was in tears as she told me. This simple habit was allowing her to watch a miracle happen.

Joshua 1:8 says, "Study this Book of Instruction continually. Meditate on it day and night so you will be sure to obey everything written in it. Only then will you prosper and succeed in all you do." Janet and Kevin are helping their children meditate on God's Word, which has buried these verses deep inside them.

When one of my sons was four, he memorized Ephesians 3:17-19 accidentally, simply because we were praying it over him as a blessing every night. One morning he began to sing the verses over his baby brother (which melted my heart). In 2022, I added a second blessing to each of my sons' bedtime routines, mostly because I wanted to memorize Titus 3:4-7 and needed the consistent time to review it. As a result of me praying these verses over them each night, all three of my sons memorized that long, beautiful (and somewhat obtuse) passage without even trying.

Better Sleep

Praying a Bible verse over our child becomes the keystone habit that ends our bedtime routine every single time, signaling to our kids that it's time to go to sleep—even as teens. Placing God's Word in their minds and hearts helps them sleep peacefully, and it helps everyone end the routine with love and kindness instead of hurry and irritation.

David and Viola have four children, two of whom were struggling with bedtime fears and nightmares. When the parents began speaking blessings over their kids, the nightmares went away. And slowly, bedtime struggles eased. Their children began to wake up happy in the morning, rather than cranky from a poor night's sleep.[4]

I have heard from *many* families that their children began to go to sleep more peacefully and stop having nightmares when the family started praying nightly blessings. For some families, the change happens within one night. Isn't that mind-boggling? It turns out that the key to good sleep is God's voice in our hearts.

Once, when my eldest was a toddler, he woke up in the middle of the night and would not go back to sleep. No amount of soothing, breastfeeding, singing, or jiggling made him rest easy. Over an hour later, I was begging God to force my baby's eyes closed when a random thought popped into my brain: *I didn't pray his blessing over him tonight.* In desperation, I spoke the priestly blessing from Numbers over him, and I kid you not, that wide-awake toddler lay down and went back to sleep instantly. The rest of my night was overtaken by shock. Over thirteen years later, I still vividly remember crawling back into my stone-cold bed and staring at the ceiling, wondering what on earth had just gone down. Somehow, some way, my little guy had been instantly comforted by God's words.

I do have one caveat to mention: A few families found that their children started sleeping *worse* after they began blessing their children nightly. They later realized that it was spiritual warfare, so after bathing the situation in prayer, they found that their children began to sleep well again. This illustrates what an incredibly powerful thing we are doing. Biblical blessings over our children have great power in the spiritual realm. If this happens to you, simply double down in prayer for your kids. Pray for protection from the enemy, who wants to steal their hearts.

Increasing Desire for God

Only God can soften hard hearts, focus a distracted child, or spray spiritual weed killer. My job is to trust, pray, and faithfully share my faith with them. When one of my boys started questioning the existence of God, I simply prayed that he would experience Christ's love, though it is too great to understand fully. I prayed Ephesians 3:17-19 over him every night for over two years before seeing any spiritual fruit in his life. But one night when he was around six, I found him in his bed, surrounded by stuffed animals, engrossed in a little notebook. He was drawing on every page. Later, he told me he had made a "God Bible." Each page showed God loving an aspect of his creation, from people to animals to books. It was like a little whisper from God to my own heart: "Don't worry, Mama; I've got him in my hands."

Praying blessings over our children puts his words on our hearts at regular times throughout our week, reminding us of his goodness. I believe that God will honor the few moments we spend blessing our children by giving us all a greater thirst for him.

Remember David and Viola? As their children started waking up well rested, their morning routine became smoother. Since they were not in such a rush each morning, they started a twenty-minute Bible reading and prayer time. They continued this morning routine for over a decade. Most of their children are now grown, and David and Viola still have very open communication with them. While their kids are unlikely to remember all the things they read, discussed, and prayed about during those years, the long-term effects of this precious time are eternal—all because they began a simple practice of blessing their children before bed.

Increasing Peace

Speaking biblical blessings over your child is a powerful way to bring God's peace into their heart and mind. Here's what happened in Lyssa's family:

> My sweet girls had been battling irrational fears at
> night. I loved your idea of bedtime blessings, so we
> implemented the one (from Ephesians) about a month
> ago, which helped with bedtime in general. All my

kiddos, even my seven-year-old son, LOVE this end to our bedtime routine and remind me every night not to forget. I added the blessing from Numbers last week, and we were able to have some great conversations about how Jesus is our Peace. Tonight my five-year-old said, "Mommy, you don't have to pray for me not to be scared anymore. I don't have to be scared because there is Peace in my room," and she pointed to the blessing. THIS. IS. HUGE. The sweet girl has wrestled with fear for a long time, and for her to say that and then just go to sleep is miraculous! So thank you for the huge impact you have had on our family (and my evening sanity)![5]

When I reached out to Lyssa for permission to share this message she had sent back in December 2018, she told me that they still do it every night:

When I go on trips, the kids call and ask me to do their blessings with them before bed. It has evolved so that each child has adopted one of the blessings as their own. This has become such a cherished routine and has helped instill the Word deeply in all our hearts.[6]

Dr. Michelle Anthony calls the nightly blessing an example of how parents can make "long-lasting deposits" into the spiritual lives of their children.[7] Praise God for his incredible goodness, taking our mustard-seed-sized faith and turning it into something beautiful for his glory.

You can bless your babies in utero, you can bless your small children, you can bless your teens, you can bless other people's children, and you can bless grown children and grandchildren.

In *The Broken Way*, Ann Voskamp writes, "You do something great with your life when you do all the small things with His great love."[8] Praying biblical blessings over your child is a very small thing, but when done with God's great love, it becomes something great and makes a difference in your child's eternal life.

IDEAS FOR PROMPTS AND REWARDS

You CAN'T CREATE A HABIT LOOP without prompts and rewards! Anchoring prompts are realistic moments in your day that help remind you to do the little behavior you chose. Rewards are ways to ensure the behavior becomes a habit, and for our family faith formation, we create rewards through instant celebrations.

While any number of things can serve as a prompt or reward, I've included a noncomprehensive list of ideas for both to help you identify what could work in your family. You may notice something here that will work as a useful anchor or celebration for you, or this list may simply help you brainstorm other anchors or celebrations to try.

ANCHOR PROMPTS

As you look through these prompt ideas, ask God, *Where can I invite you into what I'm already doing?*

Morning

- get out of bed
- turn on the shower
- brush my teeth
- turn on the coffee maker
- sit down for breakfast
- put the breakfast dishes away
- load the dishwasher
- buckle my seat belt
- pull up to the front doors of the school
- turn on my computer
- arrive at the bus stop with my kids
- see my kids put on their backpacks
- open my Bible

Afternoon

- leave church
- hear the school bell
- hear a siren
- feel hungry
- eat lunch
- feed our pet
- walk into the kitchen
- use the bathroom
- wash my hands
- find a spot in the pickup line
- pick up my kids at the bus stop
- close the door to the van when picking up my kids

Evening

- walk in the door after work
- turn on the TV
- sit down to eat dinner
- clean the kitchen counter
- walk the dog
- run the bathwater
- finish bathing my child
- pick up my child's toothbrush
- tuck my child in
- set my alarm
- put my head on my pillow

REWARDS

Celebrations for You

- smile
- breathe deeply and think, *Thank you, God!*
- whisper, "I did it!"
- whisper, "Victory!"
- pump your fist in the air
- give yourself a pat on the back

Celebrations with Your Child

- give them a hug (Bonus points if you create a special hug you only use at this moment, like a koala hug or super squeeze.)

- give them a high five or fist bump (Hot tip: Let your child give you the hardest high five they can. Some kids will *live* for this moment when you howl about how painful their high five was.)

- give each other butterfly kisses (Silly twist: Let your child find the most ticklish spot on your face with their eyelashes, and really ham up how much it tickles.)

Appendix D

ROOTED RESOURCES

IF YOU'RE LOOKING FOR THE NEXT STEP beyond the simple habits, check out hopegrownfaith.com for an entire course dedicated to going deeper in the areas of praying with kids, reading the Bible, understanding sacred pathways, and sharing the gospel in both official and organic ways with children. In addition, you'll find a two-year curriculum of simple, fun Bible studies that get your kids reading the actual Bible, having real conversations about it, and enjoying the process!

Beyond the ongoing support through HopeGrown Faith, here are a few other simple, relevant resources I can personally vouch for that will help you go deeper in one or more specific areas. My hope is that these extra resources will point you toward deeper reliance on the Holy Spirit in your parenting and that they won't feel like burdens. I've organized them into topics based on how often they come up in conversation (in person and online). Use only what's helpful for you, and remember that this isn't a required reading list!

PRAYER

Prayer can be the easiest thing to do with kids . . . but also the hardest. When you're trying to help your child develop a consistent and honest prayer life, check out the prayer lessons inside HopeGrown Faith or grab one of these resources:

Resources for You

- *Pray with Me: Help Your Children Engage in Authentic and Powerful Prayer* by Erica Renaud

- *Raising Prayerful Kids: Fun and Easy Activities for Building Lifelong Habits of Prayer* by Stephanie Thurling and Sarah Holmstrom

Resources for Your Child

- *How to Pray: A Guide for Young Explorers* by Pete Greig and Gemma Hunt

- *The Mother and Son Prayer Journal: A Keepsake Devotional to Share and Connect through God* by Christie Thomas

SCRIPTURE READING/MEMORY

It can feel intimidating to read the Bible with kids, but your child doesn't need to understand everything they hear the first time around. As quoted in *Every Season Sacred*, theologian Dietrich Bonhoeffer wrote,

> God's Word is to be heard by everyone in his own way and according to the measure of his understanding. A child hears and learns the Bible for the first time in

family worship; the adult Christian learns it repeatedly and better, and he will never finish acquiring knowledge of its story.[1]

You are invited to discover the Bible along with your child. Follow the Faith Growth Cycle to figure out a good place and time to start, but also invite God to inspire you with which part of the Bible to start with (I personally find the Gospels an excellent place). When you're trying to find a way to engage your kids more in the practice of Scripture reading, check out the Bible teaching lesson inside HopeGrown Faith, or grab these books:

Resource for You

- *Help Your Kids Learn and Love the Bible* by Danika Cooley

Resources for Your Child

- *Topical Memory System for Kids* by The Navigators (and the follow-up book, *Topical Memory System for Kids: Be Like Jesus!*)

BIBLE STORIES/DEVOTIONAL READING

There are more Bible storybooks and devotional books in the world than there is time to read them all. When I'm looking for a supplementary resource like this, I look for books that follow these basic principles:

1. **God is the hero.** The Bible is the story of God working in human history, so every devotion and Bible story must point back to God as the hero, not humans. If God (as one

or more of the persons of the Trinity) is not mentioned in each story or devotion, don't waste your time. You may learn the facts of Bible stories if you pick up a people-centered book, but your children won't be changed by a relationship with God if all they learn is Bible facts.

2. **The lessons or stories aren't moralistic.** When we read our children devotions that tell them to stop lying/grumbling/cheating/sinning or to be more respectful/loving/obedient/generous/good and then quote a verse at them to make them obedient, we are not preaching the good news of the gospel. "We know that a person is made right with God by faith in Jesus Christ, not by obeying the law. And we have believed in Christ Jesus, so that we might be made right with God because of our faith in Christ, not because we have obeyed the law. For no one will ever be made right with God by obeying the law" (Galatians 2:16). Yes, we want our children to grow in character, but obedience comes out of salvation, not as a requirement for it. Be wary of books that put too much emphasis on behavior.

Now that you have two helpful criteria for choosing a devotional or Bible storybook, you can flip through books (in person and online) and make decisions for yourself. I can't possibly list all the resources I've used, but here are two that I can vouch for:

- *Fruit Full: 100 Family Experiences for Growing in the Fruit of the Spirit* by Christie Thomas

- *My First Devotional* by Christie Thomas (forthcoming from Christian Art Gifts)

GOSPEL LIVING

"*Everything that isn't gospel is law.* Every way we try to make our kids good that isn't rooted in the good news of the life, death, resurrection, and ascension of Jesus Christ is damnable, crushing, despair-breeding, Pharisee-producing law."[2] That's a powerful way to say that we need to avoid teaching our kids to be nice, moral people at the expense of knowing where their salvation comes from. When you need inspiration for sharing the gospel with your kids, check out the gospel-sharing lesson inside HopeGrown Faith or grab one of these books:

- *Give Them Grace: Dazzling Your Kids with the Love of Jesus* by Elyse M. Fitzpatrick and Jessica Thompson

- *Gospel-Centered Mom: The Freeing Truth about What Your Kids Really Need* by Brooke McGlothlin

RACIAL ENGAGEMENT

Our kids are growing up in a culture that is beautifully diverse, and as Christians, we need to learn ways to love those who seem different from us. When you're looking for resources that will give you a big helping of grace along with the truth, as well as provide small, simple changes for your family, I highly recommend you pick up one of these as a great place to start:

- *Becoming All Things: How Small Changes Lead to Lasting Connections across Cultures* by Michelle Ami Reyes

- *The Race-Wise Family: Ten Postures to Becoming Households of Healing and Hope* by Helen Lee and Michelle Ami Reyes

APOLOGETICS

As you and your kids encounter challenges to your faith, it can be helpful to have a couple of apologetics books on hand as reference points so you are personally equipped. When you find yourself facing questions you don't know how to answer, turn to one of these books to help you out:

Resources for You

- *Mama Bear Apologetics: Empowering Your Kids to Challenge Cultural Lies* edited by Hillary Morgan Ferrer

- *Talking with Your Kids about Jesus: 30 Conversations Every Christian Parent Must Have* by Natasha Crain

Resources for Your Child

- *10 Questions Every Teen Should Ask (and Answer) about Christianity* by Rebecca McLaughlin

- *Case for Christ for Kids* by Lee Strobel with Rob Suggs and Robert Elmer (plus the other books in this series)

THE CHURCH CALENDAR

I knew nothing about the historic church calendar until recently, but as I learned about it, I felt like I'd uncovered buried treasure. In my Protestant circles, I have rarely run across someone who talks about the liturgical calendar. I knew it was there, but I didn't think it was for me. If you've ever looked for connections to the global and historic faith through ancient Jewish feasts, I highly recommend checking out these books on the liturgical calendar, as they'll help provide similar kinds of connections to the greater community of faith:

- *Every Season Sacred: Reflections, Prayers, and Invitations to Nourish Your Soul and Nurture Your Family throughout the Year* by Kayla Craig

- *Sacred Seasons: A Family Guide to Center Your Year around Jesus* by Danielle Hitchen

ACKNOWLEDGMENTS

At my grandpa's funeral, my dad shared a story I'd never heard before. Imagine an eight-year-old farm kid in the 1950s peeking through the kitchen window of his little house in rural Alberta. Through the glass, he watches his parents bow their heads at the kitchen table alongside a traveling evangelist, praying to receive Christ. Thank you to that evangelist for being part of my family faith story. You started a chain that proves our God is "the faithful God who keeps his covenant for a thousand generations and lavishes his unfailing love on those who love him and obey his commands" (Deuteronomy 7:9). Thank you to my grandparents and parents for loving God and obeying his commands, enabling me to know Christ from an early age, and thank you to God for including us in your covenant of love.

The existence of this book owes major thanks to my husband, who spent his evenings shuttling kids around or closing my office door to keep kids out. He also helped me work through several sticky spots in this book with his wise suggestions and prodding questions. Jon, I know you'll roll your eyes, but I wouldn't have been able to write this book without you as my steadfast champion in many areas of life. Obviously, our boys were important to this endeavor as well, being the perfect guinea pigs for my family Bible studies and activities. Ethan, Oliver, and Jackson—thanks for giving me the inspiration and space to write so others could be encouraged, and thank you for allowing me to share some of your story.

To the women (and occasional man) of HopeGrown Faith, thank you for taking a chance on this material while it was still in development, encouraging me as I figured out the Faith Growth Cycle concepts and shared them with you! A double thanks to those whose stories are featured in this book. I love seeing God work in your families as you are faithful with the small things.

To my friends and beta readers—Sarah, Melissa, Toni, Tina, Tambra, Nathalie, and Meshelle: Thanks for being a motivating and wise sounding board as I worked out these ideas.

Caitlyn Carlson—I don't ever want to write a book without you again. Your brilliant puzzle skills made this book so much better. And a huge, gushing *thank you* to the rest of the team at NavPress and Tyndale for believing this message was important enough to put in a book.

Finally . . . Jesus, you really are the best. You've been faithful in every big and little moment, and I can't wait to spend the rest of my life (and eternity) with you.

NOTES

INTRODUCTION | A VERY GOOD PLACE TO START

1. Ryan Coatney, accessed September 9, 2023, https://crossformedkids.com /start-here.
2. For this study of the book of Mark, see Christie Thomas, "40 Days with Jesus," https://christiethomas.ck.page/9d75944618.
3. Misty Steinloski, email conversation with author, June 7, 2023. Used with permission.

CHAPTER 1 | THE POWER OF A PARENT

1. Timothy Larsen, "When Did Sunday Schools Start?," *Christianity Today*, August 28, 2008, https://www.christianitytoday.com/history/2008/august /when-did-sunday-schools-start.html.
2. Kitchen Table Project is part of the ministry of Care for the Family, a family-faith ministry based out of the UK. "Who and What Influences Children to Develop Their Own Personal Christian Faith?," accessed May 25, 2023, http://kitchentable.org.uk/wp-content/uploads/2017/12/The-Kitchen-Table -Project-Booklet-V6-Digital.pdf.
3. Mark A. Holmen, *Building Faith at Home: Why Faith at Home Must Be Your Church's #1 Priority* (Ventura, CA: Regal Books, 2007), 26.
4. Laura Hancock, ed., *Gen Z: Rethinking Culture* (Halesowen, UK: Youth for Christ, 2016), accessed May 25, 2023, https://indd.adobe.com/view /0672cab6-cf26-4595-b572-9146f31af43e.
5. "Reasons 18- to 22-Year-Olds Drop Out of Church," Lifeway Research, August 7, 2007, https://research.lifeway.com/2007/08/07/reasons-18-to-22 -year-olds-drop-out-of-church.
6. David Briggs, "The No. 1 Reason Teens Keeps the Faith as Young Adults," *HuffPost*, October 29, 2014, https://www.huffpost.com/entry/the-no-1 -reason-teens-kee_b_6067838.

7. Jana Magruder, *Nothing Less: Engaging Kids in a Lifetime of Faith* (Nashville: Lifeway, 2017), 50.
8. Vern L. Bengtson with Norella M. Putney and Susan Harris, *Families and Faith: How Religion Is Passed Down across Generations* (New York: Oxford University Press, 2013), 79.
9. See https://littleshootsdeeproots.com/blessing-challenge.
10. Tara L. Cole, email conversation with author, June 1, 2023. Used with permission.

CHAPTER 2 | STRUGGLES AND SOLUTIONS
1. See Ezekiel 4.
2. Justin Whitmel Earley, *Habits of the Household: Practicing the Story of God in Everyday Family Rhythms* (Grand Rapids, MI: Zondervan, 2021), 61.
3. BJ Fogg, *Tiny Habits: The Small Changes That Change Everything* (New York: Mariner Books, 2020), 165.
4. Nathaniel Peters, email conversation with author, June 14, 2023. Used with permission.

CHAPTER 3 | WHAT'S MY *WHY*?
1. Vern L. Bengtson with Norella M. Putney and Susan Harris, *Families and Faith: How Religion Is Passed Down across Generations* (New York: Oxford University Press, 2013), 142.
2. Jennifer Pepito, *Mothering by the Book: The Power of Reading Aloud to Overcome Fear and Recapture Joy* (Minneapolis: Bethany House, 2022), 93.
3. Halford E. Luccock, "The Gospel according to St. Mark," in *General Articles on the New Testament; Matthew; Mark*, vol. 7 in *The Interpreter's Bible*, ed. George Arthur Buttrick (Nashville: Abingdon Press, 1951), 707.
4. See Christie Thomas, HopeGrown Faith online course, https://hopegrown faith.com.
5. Sarah Armstrong, email conversations with author, June 1, 2023. Used with permission.

CHAPTER 4 | WHAT'S GETTING IN MY WAY?
1. Timothy Keller, "Jesus on the Mount; Jesus off the Mount" (sermon audio recording), Gospel in Life, July 2, 2006, https://gospelinlife.com/downloads /jesus-on-the-mount-jesus-off-the-mount-5465.
2. Natalia Torres, Facebook Messenger conversation with author, June 1, 2023. Used with permission.

CHAPTER 5 | WHY START LITTLE?
1. Christie Thomas, *Wise for Salvation: Meaningful Devotions for Families with Little Ones* (Winnipeg: Word Alive Press, 2015).

2. Sally Clarkson, *10 Gifts of Heart: What Your Child Needs to Take to Heart before Leaving Home* (Monument, CO: Whole Heart Press, 2017), 24.

3. BJ Fogg, *Tiny Habits: The Small Changes That Change Everything* (New York: Mariner Books, 2020), 8.

4. This concept is explained in far more depth in Fogg's book *Tiny Habits*, which I highly recommend.

5. If you like to geek out about habit formation like me, check out the Fogg Behavior Model (https://behaviormodel.org), created by BJ Fogg.

6. Fogg, *Tiny Habits*, 10.

7. If you're struggling to come up with something short and specific and my list doesn't help, send me an email at christie@littleshootsdeeproots, and I'll help you come up with a version of the habit that's truly little.

8. Kelsey M. Andrews, email conversation with author, May 20, 2023. Used with permission.

CHAPTER 6 | WHERE DO I START?

1. Charles Duhigg, *The Power of Habit: Why We Do What We Do in Life and Business* (Toronto: Anchor Canada, 2014), 101.

2. The power of keystone habits is explained throughout chapter 4 of Duhigg, *Power of Habit*.

3. See Stephanie Thurling and Sarah Holmstrom, *Raising Prayerful Kids: Fun and Easy Activities for Building Lifelong Habits of Prayer* (Carol Stream, IL: Tyndale House Publishers, 2022).

4. Duhigg, *Power of Habit*, 101.

5. Heather Jolly, email conversation with author, May 15, 2023. Used with permission.

CHAPTER 7 | HOW DO I KEEP GOING?

1. This "habit equation" is found in BJ Fogg, *Tiny Habits: The Small Changes That Change Everything* (New York: Mariner Books, 2020). Again, I highly recommend reading the whole book, but you can also take a look at https://behaviormodel.org for a quick overview.

2. BJ Fogg calls these three types of prompts Person Prompts, Context Prompts, and Action Prompts and has nicknamed the Action Prompts *anchors*.

3. Fogg, *Tiny Habits*, 107.

4. James Clear, *Atomic Habits: An Easy and Proven Way to Build Good Habits and Break Bad Ones* (New York: Avery, 2018), 74.

5. Clear, *Atomic Habits*, 79.

6. Mark Rober, "The Super Mario Effect—Tricking Your Brain into Learning More | Mark Rober | TEDxPenn," TedX Talks, May 31, 2018, YouTube video, https://youtu.be/9vJRopau0g0.

7. Charles Duhigg explains that the habit loop system contains a cue, a routine, and a reward. See Charles Duhigg, *The Power of Habit: Why We Do What We Do in Life and Business* (Toronto: Anchor Canada, 2014), 19.

8. Fogg, *Tiny Habits*, 134.
9. Leah Martin, email conversation with author, May 22, 2023. Used with permission.

PART FOUR: OPENING THOUGHTS
1. Justin Whitmel Earley, *Habits of the Household: Practicing the Story of God in Everyday Family Rhythms* (Grand Rapids, MI: Zondervan, 2021), 28.

CHAPTER 8 | HOW DO I GO DEEPER?
1. Gretchen Ronnevik, "On Josh Harris, Homeschooling, and Spiritual Formulas," August 5, 2019, https://gretchenronnevik.com/2019/08 /on-josh-harris-homeschooling-and-spiritual-formulas.html.
2. In the ACTS prayer pattern, the acronym stands for *adoration, confession, thanksgiving,* and *supplication.*
3. Melissa Faulkner, email conversation with author, May 23, 2023. Used with permission.

CHAPTER 9 | HOW DO I GET THEM TO DO IT ALONE?
1. The What's in the Bible? videos are such fun, and I can guarantee that you'll learn something from them too. You can stream them online through https://www.gominno.com or find them at https://whatsinthebible.com /witb.
2. Ruth Hancock, email conversation with author, May 20, 2023. Used with permission.

CHAPTER 10 | WHAT DO I DO WHEN LIFE CHANGES?
1. Diane Unger, email conversation with author, May 30, 2023. Used with permission.

FINAL THOUGHTS
1. James Clear, *Atomic Habits: An Easy and Proven Way to Build Good Habits and Break Bad Ones* (New York: Avery, 2018), 117.
2. Jennifer Zimmerman, email conversation with author, May 22, 2023. Used with permission.

APPENDIX A | IDEAS FOR LITTLE HABITS
1. Ann Voskamp, *The Broken Way: A Daring Path into the Abundant Life* (Grand Rapids, MI: Zondervan, 2016), 75.

APPENDIX B | THE BLESSING HABIT
1. John Trent, Gary Smalley, and Kari Trent Stageberg, *The Blessing: Giving the Gift of Unconditional Love and Acceptance*, rev. ed. (Nashville: W Publishing Group, 2019), 43.

2. Trent, Smalley, and Stageberg, *The Blessing*, 44.
3. Names have been changed to protect privacy.
4. David and Viola Dueck, Facebook conversation with author, April 19, 2023. Used with permission.
5. Lyssa Rickard, Facebook conversation with author, December 2018. Used with permission.
6. Lyssa Rickard, Facebook conversation with author, May 20, 2023. Used with permission.
7. Michelle Anthony and Megan Marshman, *7 Family Ministry Essentials: A Strategy for Culture Change in Children's and Student Ministries* (Colorado Springs: David C Cook, 2015), 48.
8. Ann Voskamp, *The Broken Way: A Daring Path into the Abundant Life* (Grand Rapids, MI: Zondervan, 2016), 103.

APPENDIX D | ROOTED RESOURCES

1. Dietrich Bonhoeffer, as quoted in Kayla Craig, *Every Season Sacred: Reflections, Prayers, and Invitations to Nourish Your Soul and Nurture Your Family throughout the Year* (Carol Stream, IL: Tyndale Momentum, 2023), 5.
2. Elyse M. Fitzpatrick and Jessica Thompson, *Give Them Grace: Dazzling Your Kids with the Love of Jesus* (Wheaton, IL: Crossway, 2011), 36.